THE BEST IN TENT CAMPING:

WEST VIRGINIA

---

*A Guide for Campers Who Hate RVs, Concrete Slabs,
and Loud Portable Stereos*

D0815672

OTHER BOOKS
BY JOHNNY MOLLOY

Day & Overnight Hikes in the Monongahela National Forest

Day & Overnight Hikes in the Great Smoky Mountains National Park

Day & Overnight Hikes in Shenandoah National Park

Trial by Trail: Backpacking in the Smoky Mountains

The Best in Tent Camping: The Southern Appalachian & Smoky Mountains

The Best in Tent Camping: Florida

The Best in Tent Camping: Colorado

Beach & Coastal Camping in Florida

Paddler's Guide to Everglades National Park

THE BEST IN TENT CAMPING:

WEST VIRGINIA

---

*A Guide for Campers Who Hate RVs, Concrete Slabs,
and Loud Portable Stereos*

Johnny Molloy

Menasha
Ridge
Press, Inc.

This book is for my longtime West Virginia friend, Steve Grayson.

Library of Congress Cataloging-in-Publication Data is available
from the Library of Congress.

ISBN 0-89732-317-3

Cover design by Grant Tatum
Cover photo by Robert P. Falls, Sr.

Menasha Ridge Press
700 South 28th Street, Suite 206
Birmingham, Alabama 35233

CONTENTS

MAP LEGEND

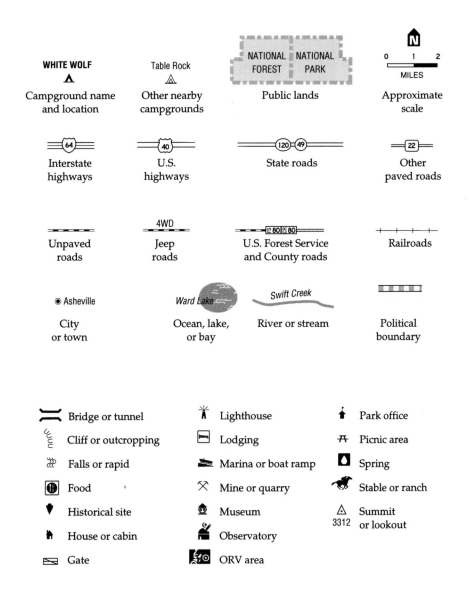

WHITE WOLF
Campground name
and location

Table Rock
Other nearby
campgrounds

NATIONAL NATIONAL
FOREST PARK
Public lands

0   1   2
MILES
Approximate
scale

64
Interstate
highways

40
U.S.
highways

120 49
State roads

22
Other
paved roads

Unpaved
roads

4WD
Jeep
roads

80 80
U.S. Forest Service
and County roads

Railroads

● Asheville
City
or town

Ward Lake
Ocean, lake,
or bay

Swift Creek
River or stream

Political
boundary

Bridge or tunnel

Cliff or outcropping

Falls or rapid

Food

Historical site

House or cabin

Gate

Lighthouse

Lodging

Marina or boat ramp

Mine or quarry

Museum

Observatory

ORV area

Park office

Picnic area

Spring

Stable or ranch

Summit
3312 or lookout

Allegheny Highlands
1. Bear Heaven
2. Bishop Knob
3. Blue Bend
4. Cranberry
5. Day Run
6. Horseshoe Run
7. Island
8. Kumbrabrow State Forest
9. Lake Sherwood
10. Laurel Fork
11. Pocahontas
12. Seneca State Forest
13. Spruce Knob Lake
14. Summit Lake
15. Tea Creek
16. Watoga State Park

Eastern Panhandle
17. Big Bend
18. Blackwater Falls State Park
19. Brandywine Lake
20. Camp Run
21. Hawk
22. Red Creek
23. Seneca Shadows
24. Sleepy Creek
25. Trout Pond
26. Wolf Gap

Feudin' Country
27. Beech Fork State Park
28. Cabwaylingo State Forest
29. Chief Logan State Park
30. Kanawah State Forest
31. Panther State Forest
32. R. D. Bailey Lake

Heart of West Virginia
33. Audra State Park
34. Bakers Run
35. Bulltown

36. Cedar Creek State Park
37. Coopers Rock State Forest
38. Holly River State Park
39. Pleasant Creek WMA

New River Valley
40. Army Camp
41. Babcock State Park
42. Bluestone State Park
43. Camp Creek State Park and Forest
44. Glade Creek
45. Greenbriar River State Forest
46. Moncove Lake State Park

Ohio River Valley
47. Lewis Wetzel
48. McClintic WMA
49. North Bend State Park
50. Tomlinson Run State Park

ACKNOWLEDGMENTS

I would like to thank the following people for helping me in the research and writing of this book: Robert and Bonnie Gross, Roxanna Carr, Roy Reynolds, Jat Hedrick, Anna Galenza at Bulltown, Karen Stokes, Cindy Thomas, Mike Foster, and Cindy Blair. Thanks to Frank Sellars for his information on the New River, and to Stephanie Bailey and Barbara Breshock for getting questioned during their lunch. Thanks to John Markwell at the Gendarme in Seneca Rocks for his advice about the area. Thanks to Dale A. Porter for his books and information. Thanks to Keith Stinnett, Deal Holcomb, Cisco Meyer, Nelle Molloy, Steele Molloy, and Pat Molloy for the Jeep bailout. And thanks to Mr. Dash — Dave Zaczyk.

Thanks to Eureka for providing me with a great tent, the Timberline, for camping; Silva compasses; and Camp Trails for their Daily Grind day pack. Thanks to Caroline Fleischer at Freebairn & Co., and to Slumberjack for a good sleeping bag and sleeping mat to enable a good night's rest. Thanks to Outdoor Outfitters for getting me other equipment I needed.

The biggest thanks of all goes to the people of West Virginia, who love their mountain lands.

PREFACE

With a Jeep, a laptop computer, and an open mind I set forth into the hills of West Virginia. The first trip started in the spring. In southwest Virginia, historic coal country, I came upon my first surprise, Panther State Forest. The place was covered in wildflowers! It started raining the next morning. Such are times that a tent camper has to face. Next I headed up the valley of the river Ohio. Amidst the development along the waterway, I found other gems such as Tomlinson Run, where the trees of the hilltop campground hadn't begun to leaf out, and I spent a cold night as the sole occupant of the campground.

More trips extended into the summer. As the weather warmed in the "low-lands" around me, the Alleghenies and lake areas became the places to go. The weather was great and the scenery even better. Getaways like Bulltown, an Army Corps of Engineers' preserve, offered glimpses into the vast human history of the Mountain State, as well as a watery place to cool off. Other times I headed high into the Monongahela National Forest, to places like Bear Heaven, where on July evenings I donned a jacket and scooted a little closer to the campfire.

The more campgrounds I visited, the more I appreciated the people who operated these preserves. They were hardworking, enthusiastic patrons of their lands. Sometimes the park staff was better than the campground, and it was disappointing not to include these campgrounds in the book.

The days began to shorten—fall was on its way. There were still more campgrounds to inspect. This was when I headed down to the New River area. I had rafted the river, as well as the Gauley, in previous years and knew how scenic these gorges were. I enjoyed Glade Creek, part of the New River National Recreation Area, so much, I went back for a second visit, under the guise of "making sure" it should be in the book.

And with the joy of completing a book and the sadness of an adventure ended, I finished my research. But, not surprisingly, within a month of turning in the manuscript, I had returned with a friend to the Dolly Sods for a backpacking trip and to the upper New River for a canoe trip. And so I shall return to the Mountain State for years to come. So will you.

—Johnny Molloy

THE BEST IN TENT CAMPING:

WEST VIRGINIA

*A Guide for Campers Who Hate RVs, Concrete Slabs,
and Loud Portable Stereos*

INTRODUCTION

A Word about This Book and West Virginia Tent Camping

West Virginia is an unusual state. Born of the Civil War, culled from the Old Dominion, it has been called the northernmost Southern state, or the southernmost northern state. Its nickname is the Mountain State, and mountainous it is. It's been said that if the ridges and peaks of West Virginia were flattened out, it would be the size of Texas. It has the highest average elevation of any state east of the Mississippi River. Straight roads and flat lands are few and far between.

I call it the most untapped natural resource in the East. If the United States was as preservation minded 150 years ago as it is today, we might have West Virginia National Park. This state is that beautiful. But progress and people came (not a bad thing) and settled what was then Old Virginia, building lives and communities in the hollows along streams and rivers. West Virginia became a state, and special places began to be set aside for nature to dominate.

Today tent campers can enjoy these parcels, pieces of each distinct region of West Virginia. In Feudin' Country, so named after the infamous Hatfield-McCoy quarrels of yesteryear, you can explore the most hilly terrain of the Mountain State, or any other state for that matter. The Ohio River Valley is the land of frontiersmen and Indians, where history was played out as the human tide swept westward. The New River Gorge is home to one of the continent's oldest rivers, which has cut a scenic swath through the ridges of coal country. The Heart of West Virginia is a region of lakes, where numerous reservoirs offer water recreation. The Allegheny Highlands have the highest elevations and most diverse forests, crowned with dark stands of red spruce. The Eastern Panhandle has the drier pine/oak/hickory highlands interspersed with rock outcrops offering scenic views of valleys below.

All this spells paradise for the tent camper. No matter where you go, the scenery will never fail to please. Before embarking on a trip, take time to prepare. Many of the best tent campgrounds are a fair distance from the civilized world, and you want to enjoy yourself rather than make supply or gear runs. Call ahead and ask for a park map, brochure, or other information to help you plan your trip. Visit the campground's or park's Web site if it has one. Make reservations wherever possible, especially at popular state parks. Ask questions.

Then ask more questions. The more you ask, the fewer surprises you'll find. There are other times, however, when you'll grab your gear and this book, hop in the car, and just wing it. This can be an adventure in its own right.

The rating system

Included in this book is a rating system for West Virginia's 50 best tent campgrounds. Certain campground attributes—beauty, site privacy, site spaciousness, quiet, security, and cleanliness/upkeep—are ranked using a star system. Five stars are ideal, one is acceptable. This system will help you find the campground that has the attributes you desire.

Beauty

In the best campgrounds, the fluid shapes and elements of nature—flora, water, land, and sky—have melded to create locales that seem to have been made for tent camping. The best sites are so attractive you may be tempted not to leave your outdoor home. A little site work is all right to make the scenic area camper-friendly, but too many reminders of civilization eliminated many a campground from inclusion in this book.

Site privacy

A little understory goes a long way in making you feel comfortable once you've picked your site for the night. There is a trend in planting natural borders between campsites if the borders don't exist already. With some trees or brush to define the sites, everyone has personal space. Then you can go about the pleasures of tent camping without keeping up with the Joneses at the site next door—or them with you.

Site spaciousness

This attribute can be very important depending on how much of a gearhead you are and the size of your group. Campers with family-style tents need a large, flat spot on which to pitch their tent and still get to the ice chest to prepare foods, all the while not getting burned near the fire ring. Gearheads need adequate space to show off all their stuff to neighbors strolling by. I just want enough room to keep my bedroom, den, and kitchen separate.

Quiet

The music of the mountains—the singing birds, rushing streams, windblown meadows and trees—includes the kinds of noises tent campers associate with being in West Virginia. In concert, they camouflage the sounds you don't want to hear—autos coming and going, loud neighbors, and so on.

Security

Campground security is relative. A remote campground is usually safe, but don't tempt potential thieves by leaving your valuables out for all to see. Use common sense, and go with your instinct. Campground hosts are wonderful to have around, and state parks with locked gates are ideal for security. Get to know your neighbors and develop a buddy system to watch each other's belongings when possible.

Cleanliness/upkeep

I'm a stickler for this one. Nothing will sabotage a scenic campground like trash. Most of the campgrounds in this guidebook are clean. More rustic campgrounds—my favorites—usually receive less maintenance. Busy weekends and holidays will show their effects; however, don't let a little litter spoil your good time. Help clean up, and think of it as doing your part for West Virginia's natural environment.

Helpful hints

To make the most of your tent camping trip, call ahead whenever possible. If going to a state or national park, call for an informative brochure before setting out; this way you can familiarize yourself with the area. Once there, ask questions. Most stewards of the land are proud of their piece of terra firma and are honored you came for a visit. They're happy to help you have the best time possible.

If traveling to the Monongahela National Forest, call ahead and order a forest map. The main number is (304) 636-1800. Not only will a map make it that much easier to reach your destination, but nearby hikes, scenic drives, waterfalls, and landmarks will be easier to find. There are forest visitor centers in addition to ranger stations. Call or visit and ask questions. When ordering a map, ask for any additional literature about the area in which you are interested.

In writing this book I had the pleasure of meeting many friendly, helpful people: local residents proud of their West Virginia mountains, state park and national forest employees who endured my endless questions. Even better were my fellow tent campers, who were eager to share their knowledge about their favorite spots. They already know what a lovely place West Virginia is. As the splendor of the Mountain State becomes more recognized, these lands become that much more precious. Enjoy them, protect them, and use them wisely.

ALLEGHENY HIGHLANDS

BEAR HEAVEN

Elkins

Bear Heaven lies on a spur ridge high on Shavers Mountain outside Elkins. It can be pretty cool on summer nights. I can only imagine what the year-round campground is like around dark in mid-January. Most tent campers will head up this way during the warmer months to enjoy a small, quiet campground tucked away on the back side of the Otter Creek Wilderness.

The Otter Creek drainage forms the centerpiece of this preserved national forest land. Mountain ridges are the borders, where spruce stands and bogs hold strong. Lower in the wilderness are tangles of rhododendron over which grow northern hardwood species such as cherry and yellow birch. This area was once logged—any trails follow old railroad grades. In other areas, apple trees mark homesites long since abandoned. On the edge of the wilderness, Bear Heaven campground awaits your arrival.

What does this mean for you? It means a great place to get into the heart of natural West Virginia, where the woods are king once again. Then, you can return to your ridgetop camp and reflect on the day's observations. One of those observations will be what a fitting campground to be adjacent to the Otter Creek Wilderness. Another observation might literally be an observation—from atop the jumbled rock outcrop near the campground picnic area where you can look south over a sea of wooded ridges.

CAMPGROUND RATINGS

Beauty:	★★★★★
Site privacy:	★★★
Site spaciousness:	★★★★
Quiet:	★★★★★
Security:	★★★
Cleanliness/upkeep:	★★★★

The 20,000-acre Otter Cree Wilderness is just minutes awa from this small, secluded camp ground with a great view

ALLEGHENY HIGHLANDS

Leave the spur road off Stuart Memorial Drive and enter Bear Heaven Recreation Area. To your right is the picnic area and rock outcrop. This spur ridge is level by mountain standards and covered in a northern hardwood forest dominated by beech and cherry trees. The canopy thickens in summer, with an understory of sugar maple and striped maple. Come winter, you can better see the numerous gray boulders strewn about the campground like childrens' toy blocks tossed around a room.

Three sites occupy the main road. Wood log borders keep campers where they ought to be. The campsites are very dispersed and large, even though this spur ridge is narrow. There are winter views into the woods below. Some less-than-level sites have tent pads.

Enter a five-campsite loop. Campsites #4 and #5, the two prettiest and most used, are integrated into the boulder-dominated landscape. Swing around the loop and pass the final few campsites. This small campground has only eight units, offering the good and bad of small campgrounds: intimate, yet possibly packed with campers, as well. Bear Heaven fills during mid-summer weekends and traditional summer holidays. Other than that you should have no problem getting a campsite.

There are no trails leaving directly from the campground, other than the short walk to the rock outcrop by the picnic area, but there is a whole wilderness just to the north. Less than a mile away, on Forest Road 303, which you passed on the way in, lies the main trailhead for the southern side of the Otter Creek Wilderness. The area's 20,000 acres of rocky ridges and rhododendron-lined creeks thrive, along with the wildlife, under wilderness protection since 1975.

Here, you can start the upper end of the Otter Creek Trail. This 11-mile footpath is the backbone of the trail system. Several loop hikes can be made using a combination of trails. One circuit starts north down the Otter Creek Trail and turns right on the Mylius Gap Trail. Climb up to Mylius Gap, then turn right on the Shavers Mountain Trail and follow it for 4.3 miles to the Hedrick Camp Trail. Turn right here and you'll soon intersect the Otter Creek Trail for a 9.4-mile loop.

Or start at the top of Otter Creek Trail and walk 4.4 miles down to Pothole Falls, Otter Creek's tallest fall. Then return the way you came. To stay in the high country, start at Alpena Gap, near U.S. 33 and walk out along Shavers Mountain Trail.

Even as remote as Bear Heaven seems, the fully equipped town of Elkins is just 10 miles away, in case you need supplies or any civilized trappings. Between Elkins and Bear Heaven is the Bowden Fish Hatchery. If you have never visited a hatchery, check it out. There are fish of all sizes swimming in the tanks. It may inspire you take a rod down to Otter Creek and toss a line for the native brook trout lying secretively in the cool pools. Then you can return up to your mountaintop camp called Bear Heaven.

To get there: From Elkins, drive east on U.S. 33 for 11.5 miles to Stuart Memorial Drive, FS 91, at Alpena Gap on Shavers Mountain. Turn left on FS 91 and follow it for 1.1 miles, then veer left, staying on FS 91. Continue on FS 91 for 1.5 miles to Bear Heaven Campground, which will be on your left.

KEY INFORMATION

Bear Heaven
P.O. Box 368
Parsons, WV 26287

Operated by: U.S. Forest Service

Information: (304) 478-3251, www.fs.fed.us/r9/mon/

Open: Year-round

Individual sites: 8

Each site has: Picnic table, fire grate, lantern post

Site assignment: First come, first served; no reservations

Registration: Self-registration on site

Facilities: Pump well, vault toilets

Parking: At campsites only

Fee: $5 per night

Elevation: 3,600 feet

Restrictions:

Pets—On leash only

Fires—In fire grates only

Alcoholic beverages—At campsites only

Vehicles—None

Other—14-day stay limit

BISHOP KNOB

Richwood

Bishop Knob is an underutilized resource of the Monongahela National Forest. Other nearby campgrounds draw the crowds, leaving Bishop Knob to languish in obscurity. Don't pass this place by—and for two bucks what have you got to lose? Especially considering the assets of Bishop Knob and the other attractions that draw campers to the more popular campgrounds nearby.

So what's at Bishop Knob? Try a quiet and secluded ridgetop camping area with a few trails of its own and quick access to both the Williams and Cranberry rivers. Plus, Bishop Knob rarely gets over 50% capacity, which means you can nab a campsite already rife with natural privacy and make it even more private by having no one on either side of you. I stayed here on a July Saturday with nary a soul within five campsites of me in any direction!

The 55 campsites are divided among two loops. Turn left into the first loop. Situated in a dense hardwood forest of maple and oak, the gravel road leading through it is wide and the campsites are spread far apart. Thick undergrowth gives the level areas a greater sense of privacy, and mown edges along the gravel road and campsites add neatness to the campground. Most of the campsites are on the outside of the loop, with one pump well and two sets of vault toilets for each of the two loops.

CAMPGROUND RATINGS

Beauty: ★★★
Site privacy: ★★★★
Site spaciousness: ★★★
Quiet: ★★★★★
Security: ★★★
Cleanliness/upkeep: ★★★★

Bishop Knob is a value for all tent campers.

ALLEGHENY HIGHLANDS

The second loop is much like the first, except it has more vertical variation and meanders a bit. There are also several double campsites for larger groups or families. Most of the campsites are very appealing and don't have the beaten down look of some heavily used campgrounds. This second loop is more popular, though it's hard to figure out why. The campground as a whole is large but doesn't seem crowded; rather, it feels forgotten.

And the scenery is as appealing as anywhere in the national forest. Take a look around on the Bishop Knob Loop Trail that makes a 2-mile circuit of the campground. Start your walk near the campground pay station toward Forest Road 101 and turn right at a trail sign. Walk the serene woods to intersect the Cranberry Ridge Trail and turn right again, following the Cranberry Ridge Trail for a distance back to the loop trail. Turn right again, then pass over the dam of a pond just before returning to the campground.

Further trekking on the Cranberry Ridge Trail away from the loop hike will take you 3 miles one-way to a pretty pond on the upper stretch of Glade Run. On the drive into the campground, near the turn onto FS 101, you passed the fenced Black Cherry Seed Orchard. The Forest Service is breeding a superior strain of black cherry trees here for planting in other areas of the forest. The Adkins Rockhouse Trail starts near the orchard. You can take the Adkins Rockhouse Trail 2 miles down to the Gauley River and some good swimming holes.

The Williams and Cranberry Rivers are also just a few miles away by auto. Along these watercourses are quality trout fishing, but even if you don't catch one, you will have had an eyeful of pretty riverine sights. And if you want a view from on high, head over to Red Oak Knob, where a fire tower stands at 3,707 feet. Drive just a short distance down FS 101 from the campground to Forest Road 82. FS 82 may or may not be gated. It is a 3-mile trek from the gate that is more than worth the effort if you do have to walk.

The trip to Red Oak Knob fire tower also makes a great bike ride from the Bishop Knob. Sometimes the fire tower is open, sometimes not, but you can still climb the steps to just below the observation room for a good look over the Cranberry and Williams River Valleys. Either way, your $2 investment will have paid dividends.

To get there: From Richwood, drive east on WV 39/55 for 0.5 mile to Cranberry Road (FS 76). Turn left on Cranberry Road and follow it for nearly 3 miles to a signed intersection. FS 76 veers left and is the only gravel road at this intersection. Follow FS 76 for 4 miles to FS 81. Turn left on FS 81 and follow it for 6 miles to FS 101. Turn right on FS 101 and follow it for 0.1 mile to Bishop Knob Campground, which will be on your right.

KEY INFORMATION

Bishop Knob
Box 110
Richwood, WV 26261

Operated by: U.S. Forest Service

Information: (304) 846-2695, www.fs.fed.us/r9/mon/

Open: Mid-April through November

Individual sites: 55

Each site has: Picnic table, fire grate, lantern post

Site assignment: First come, first served; no reservations

Registration: Self-registration on site

Facilities: Pump well, vault toilets

Parking: At campsites only

Fee: $2 per night

Elevation: 3,100 feet

Restrictions:

Pets—On leash only

Fires—In fire grates only

Alcoholic beverages—At campsites only

Vehicles—None

Other—14-day stay limit

BLUE BEND

White Sulphur Springs

Blue Bend is named for a deep blue swimming hole in Anthony Creek, which flows right past the campground. This was probably a favorite cooling-off spot long before the Civilian Conservation Corps developed this campground during the Great Depression. It is still a great place to swim; Blue Bend Campground has evolved into a place where campers return time and again to pitch their tents under the tall hemlock forest. The forest service also has a great system of trails in the immediate area. There are also forest drives leading to attractive sights in the vicinity.

Pass the pay station and drop into a very thick forest of towering hemlocks on a gravel road. Rhododendron forms the primary understory, which makes for good campsite privacy. On your left is the first rest room facility. There are campsites on both sides of the road. Anthony Creek flows off in the distance, with eight campsites lined up along the creek.

The CCC did a good job of spreading out the campsites. Wood borders delineate the camping areas. White pine, tulip poplar, and maple complement the abundance of hemlocks. Some of the campsites are set far from the road, so you have to walk a bit to get to your picnic table and fire ring. These sites are generally the most private.

Come to a small turnaround loop with more hardwoods. Three campsites spoke off the turnaround. Two are directly

CAMPGROUND RATINGS

Beauty:	★★★★
Site privacy:	★★★★
Site spaciousness:	★★★★
Quiet:	★★★★
Security:	★★★★
Cleanliness/upkeep:	★★★★

Blue Bend is an old-time, old-fashioned campground first built by the Civilian Conservation Corps in the 1930s.

ALLEGHENY HIGHLANDS

streamside. These are the most coveted campsites at Blue Bend.

The number of campsites at Blue Bend, 22, is almost ideal. It's large enough that all the sites aren't constantly taken, but it's not so big you feel like you are in a tent suburb. First come, first serve means taking chances, but apart from the summer holidays, you should be able to get a campsite at 6 p.m. on Friday, if not noon on Saturday, during high summer. Blue Bend is open year-round. You'll have no trouble

finding a campsite during the shoulder seasons or winter. In fact, September would be a good time to come. The crowds are mostly gone, but the creek is still warm enough to swim. And creek swimming is the best.

The CCC built stone, patio beaches on either side of the Blue Bend. These spots are good for relaxing streamside. You can access the far side of the Blue Bend via a wooden swinging bridge. The patio on this side of the bridge has woods grown up all around. It is fun, however, to cross over the bridge and swim across to the main patio beach.

Anthony Creek is also good for trout and smallmouth bass fishing. The waterway is stocked regularly with trout during spring. Anthony Creek flows into the Greenbrier River, which is a noted smallmouth bass fishery. The Greenbrier is also known for the 75-mile Greenbrier River Rail Trail. Mountain bikers like to pedal this path of forested straightaways, curves, and bridges along the Greenbrier River.

Blue Bend has its own set of trails. The Blue Bend Loop Trail is 5 miles long, enough to justify a good, long dip in Anthony Creek after you complete the hike. Cross the swinging bridge and head downstream until you come to the

Anthony Creek Trail at mile 1.6. Turn left and climb up the side of Round Mountain, coming to a backpacking shelter at 2.7 miles. Cross over Round Mountain and drop back down to Anthony Creek, passing some overlooks facing north. Cross back over the swinging bridge to end your loop.

Anglers will want to continue down the Anthony Creek Trail from its junction with the Blue Bend Loop Trail. The Anthony Creek Trail parallels the stream for 3 more miles to the South Boundary Trail. You can continue on the Anthony Creek Trail to the Greenbrier River, but it necessitates a ford of Anthony Creek. Most hikers will return 4.6 miles to the campground. Hard-core hikers can head up the South Boundary Trail for 5 miles to Big Draft Road, then 3.5 miles on Big Draft Road, then another 1.1 miles back to Blue Bend for a blistering 14-miler.

You may want to consider touring by car instead. Just across from the campground entrance is Forest Road 139. It leads 3.5 miles up to Hopkins Lookout at 3,294 feet. Here you can get mountaintop vistas of Little Creek Valley without all the effort. Or you can go left out of the campground and follow Anthony Creek Road 4 miles to the Gunpowder Overlook. Below is the Greenbrier River and Anthony Creek Gorge. Around Blue Bend it seems everywhere you look there is attractive mountain scenery.

To get there: From White Sulphur Springs, travel north on WV 92 for 9 miles to CR 16 (Little Creek Road). Turn left on CR 16 and follow it 2 miles to CR 16/2 (Blue Bend Road). Continue forward on CR 16/2 and come to Blue Bend Campground on your left in 2 more miles.

KEY INFORMATION

Blue Bend
410 East Main Street
White Sulphur Springs, WV
24986

Operated by: U.S. Forest Service

Information: (304) 536-2144, www.fs.fed.us/r9/mon/

Open: Year-round

Individual sites: 22

Each site has: Picnic table, fire ring, lantern post

Site assignment: First come, first served, no reservations

Registration: Self-registration on site

Facilities: Flush toilets, water spigots

Parking: At campsites only

Fee: $7 per night

Elevation: 1,950 feet

Restrictions

Pets—On leash only

Fires—In fire rings only

Alcoholic beverages—At campsites only

Vehicles—None

Other—14-day stay limit

CRANBERRY

Richwood

Cranberry Campground lies in a valley at the confluence of Mill Branch and the Cranberry River. This flat was once settled and farmed by early pioneers before West Virginia was a state. The area retains some pastoral character, yet is surrounded by wild wooded mountains. Just a walk away is the Cranberry Backcountry, a good setting for hiking, biking, and fishing. When you're done exploring the Cranberry Backcountry you can return to this quiet little valley campground. And if you're lucky you'll return to one of the two walk-in tent campsites or any other campsite for that matter. Cranberry fills nearly every summer weekend.

As you follow the Cranberry River deep into the wooded mountains, suddenly the brightness of the partially open campground grabs your attention. Pass the fee station and pump well, then pull into the row of campsites to your right. These are situated in a pretty flat, broken by hemlock, rhododendron, and maples. Mown grassy areas and laid out timbers add a landscaped, organized quality to the area. The campsites are large and well separated. Up on a hill to your left are the Cranberry Graves, which is the old cemetery of the early valley settlers. A couple of more campsites lie at the end of the row just before it comes to the Cranberry Backcountry trailhead.

CAMPGROUND RATINGS

Beauty:	★★★
Site privacy:	★★★
Site spaciousness:	★★★★
Quiet:	★★★
Security:	★★★
Cleanliness/upkeep:	★★★

This campground is the gateway to the Cranberry Backcountry, haven for hikers, bikers, and anglers.

ALLEGHENY HIGHLANDS

The main campground loop passes the fee station, a couple of campsites, then crosses often dry Mill Branch on a bridge. The area here is much more open and sunny, with occasional trees on the inside of the loop. The outer part of the loop is heavily wooded. This is where the walk-in tent sites are. Park your auto, then walk across a small footbridge over Mill Branch. Come to two very shaded and secluded campsites along Mill Branch that are the best in tent camping here. They have the normal campsite amenities, plus distance from the road.

Other campsites lie back on the main loop. These are very large and offer a wide array of sun and shade situations, punctuated with brush along Mill Branch, which bisects the loop. The campsites get larger as the loop swings around toward the Cranberry River. The sites are usually occupied by pop-ups and bigger rigs. Don't camp here.

However, come here, find a good site, then explore the Cranberry Backcountry. Your main avenue of exploration is the gated Forest Road 76. It parallels the Cranberry River beyond the campground and goes on for 16 miles all the way to the Cranberry Glades Botanical Area. No private cars are allowed. Technically, the road changes to Forest Road 102, but aesthetically it only gets prettier as you head upriver. Along the way are trail shelters and numerous hiking and fishing opportunities.

Anglers will be pleased to know the Cranberry River is stocked with catchable sized trout January through May and twice in autumn. The river averages 50 feet in width. Fishing can be good on the roadside sections of the Cranberry River, too.

Make a great 9-mile loop in the Cranberry Backcountry from the campground following FS 76 for 2 miles, then turning left on the Lick Branch Trail (Forest Trail #212). Begin to look for signs of an old lumber camp as the trail climbs alongside many small falls for 2 miles to the North-South Trail (Forest Trail #688). Turn left and follow the North-South Trail along the ridge until it drops off the mountainside and returns to the Cranberry River and the campground.

Bikers take note: The Cranberry Backcountry has many wilderness qualities, yet it is not a designated wilderness, which means you can enjoy the trails of the Cranberry Backcountry as well. FS 76 makes a great treadway for pedaling, but don't wreck while enjoying that tumbling riverside scenery. The side trails aren't as biker friendly, but there is another gated road paralleling Dogway Fork (Forest Road 78) that adds enough mileage to exhaust you. FS 78 spurs off FS 76 at 6 miles. Get a forest map and go have a ball!

To get there: From Richwood, drive east on WV 39/55 for 0.5 mile to Cranberry Road (FS 76). Turn left on Cranberry Road and follow it for nearly 3 miles to an intersection. FS 76 veers left and is the only gravel road at this intersection. Follow FS 76 for 9 miles to Cranberry Campground, which will be on your left just before the road dead-ends.

KEY INFORMATION

Cranberry Campground
Box 110, Richwood, WV 26261

Operated by: U.S. Forest Service

Information: (304) 846-2695, www.fs.fed.us/r9/mon/

Open: Mid-March through early December

Individual sites: 30

Each site has: Picnic table, fire grate, lantern post

Site assignment: First come, first served; no reservations

Registration: Self-registration on site

Facilities: Pump well, vault toilets

Parking: At campsites and at walk-in tent camping area

Fee: $5 per night at sites 1–9 from March 15–July 15, $8 per night from July 16–December 8; $5 per night from March 15–December 8 at sites 10–30

Elevation: 2,500 feet

Restrictions

  Pets—On leash only

  Fires—In fire grates only

  Alcoholic beverages—At campsites only

  Vehicles—None

  Other—14-day stay limit

DAY RUN

Marlinton

The major attraction at Day Run Campground is the upper Williams River. Here, you can fish for trout or take a dip in the cool mountain waters. Outside of that, you have to get in an auto to reach other attractions, such as the Cranberry Wilderness, the Highland Scenic Highway, the Cranberry Visitor Center, the view from High Rocks, the Cranberry Glades, and the Falls of Hills Creek. Day Run, a small, secluded campground, allows access to all these attractions, yet has that slow-moving, old-time national forest campground ambiance.

Day Run is situated in a flat alongside Williams River. I'd bet this flat was once settled. It's too level and too open not to have been a farm long ago. Even so, Day Run is an old campground. Rocks and posts delineate the campsites, which support an interesting array of vegetation. Hawthorn, buckeye, sumac, crab apple, and ash grow between the grass and brush areas. Pass the fee station on a gravel road and campsite #1 is on your left, beneath some trees next to a grassy area by the pump well. Across the gravel road you'll find campsite #2 in a deep riverine woodland alongside Williams River. On your right, pass vault toilets for each gender. Across from this is campsite #3, shaded by a large crab apple tree.

Trees and brush conspire to keep campers' privacy at a maximum, especially at

CAMPGROUND RATINGS

Beauty: ★★★★
Site privacy: ★★★★★
Site spaciousness: ★★★★★
Quiet: ★★★★
Security: ★★★
Cleanliness/upkeep: ★★★

Stay in this quiet locale and enjoy the Cranberry Wilderness among other nearby forest features.

ALLEGHENY HIGHLANDS

campsites #4, 5, and 6. Number 5 is possibly the best of this bunch—a large area located near the river. Campsite #7 is also by the river, but more out in the open.

A turnaround loop begins past campsite #7. Along the loop are more examples of sun and shade mixtures to suit most any tent camper. I stayed at campsite #9—mostly sunny yet nicely shaded by a huge crab apple tree. I'd been rained on the night before and dried my wet gear in the sun while relaxing beneath the old crab apple. This site has a footpath leading to the Williams River, as do other riverside campsites here. The last three campsites offer more varieties of sun and shade plus a whole lot of privacy. Near campsite #12 is another set of vault toilets.

The small size of this campground makes for a serene setting, and the lesser developed, rustic nature of Day Run deters most big rigs. Enjoy this campground almost any weekend, except during summer holidays.

Get a Monongahela National Forest map before you come to Day Run, to get yourself on the right roads and trails. There are many attractions here, but they are spread out. Your first trip should be to the Cranberry Visitor Center. Here, you can check out the interpretive displays and figure out what is most appealing. A drive on the Highland Scenic Highway is a sure thing. Stop at some of the numerous overlooks to gaze at the mountains and valleys below. There are also trails that will reward you with even more spectacular views. The Black Mountain Trail makes a 4.6-mile loop through the high country, or try the High Rocks Trail for a truly first-rate view. It takes you on a 3.2-mile out-and-back hike that looks east toward old Virginia.

Several other trails spur off Highlands Scenic Highway into the Cranberry Wilderness. The Forks of the Cranberry Trail leads 2.1 miles to a rocky vista. Check out the Cranberry Glades for a look at a tundra environment, unique this far south. A half-mile boardwalk traverses the open bogs of the glades. For a water experience go to the Falls of Hills Creek Scenic Area. Here, a trail traces three picturesque waterfalls along Hills Creek. This walk is especially dramatic after a rain. And sure to return you to your little campground on Williams River feeling fulfilled.

To get there: From Marlinton, drive north on U.S. 210 for 7 miles to Highland Scenic Highway. Turn left on Highland Scenic Highway and follow it south for 10 miles to FS 86. Head south on FS 86 for 3 miles to FS 216. Turn right on FS 216 and follow it 1 mile to Day Run Campground, which will be on your left.

KEY INFORMATION

Day Run Campground
P.O. Box 210
Marlinton, WV 24954

Operated by: U.S. Forest Service

Information: (304) 799-4334, www.fs.fed.us/r9/mon/

Open: March 15 through December 15

Individual sites: 12

Each site has: Picnic table, fire grate, lantern post, waste can

Site assignment: First come, first served; no reservations

Registration: Self-registration on site

Facilities: Pump well, vault toilets

Parking: At campsites only

Fee: $6 per night

Elevation: 3,100 feet

Restrictions

Pets—On leash only

Fire—In fire grates only

Alcoholic beverages—At campsites only

Vehicle—None

Other—14-day stay limit

HORSESHOE RUN

Parsons

This is the kind of well-landscaped campground that makes the most of its natural setting and ends up making other campgrounds look bad. The campground is open but not too sunny. The campsites are neat but not overdone. Horseshoe Run sings its way downstream, while the mountainside across the campground rises high above Horseshoe Run. Wood smoke curls through the large white pines.

Once there was a 13-site loop and a picnic area at Horseshoe. The original loop itself was worthy of making this book, but then the powers that be turned the old picnic area into a walk-in tent camper's camp! The creekside setting is near ideal for tent campers—plenty of privacy yet convenient to campground amenities and your car. The tent campers' area made Horseshoe Campground even better and is a must for anyone tent camping in the upper Cheat River area.

This is an all-inclusive recreation area that should keep you entertained, that is, if you enjoy mountain streams, hiking trails, and canoe trips.

The entrance road drops down to flat land alongside Horseshoe Run. The neatness of the campground is immediately evident. An open grassy area lies in the center of the main loop, which is ringed by towering white pines. Smaller trees, such as yellow birch and some rhododendron, provide an understory. A lower wooded

CAMPGROUND RATINGS

Beauty:	★★★★★
Site privacy:	★★★
Site spaciousness:	★★★★
Quiet:	★★★
Security:	★★★★
Cleanliness/upkeep:	★★★★

The primary camping area is nice, but the tent campers' area is even better.

21

ALLEGHENY HIGHLANDS

flat lies between the campground and Horseshoe Run. Pass the pay station, and the campsites begin. A campground host is there for the well-being of all campers and elevated tent pads filled with small gravel mean dry sleeping even when it's raining.

The campground is twice the size it could be for so few sites. Most any combination of sun and shade is there for your taking. Most sites are first come, first served, but three sites are available for reservation. A pair of modern vault toilets are stationed between campsites #8 and #9. A footbridge crosses McKinley Run into a large field next to the campground. Kids run and play on the grass. Older kids throw the Frisbee. Others lie in the sun by the creek. The final sites continue along McKinley Run and the loop ends.

Turn left and drive to the tent camper's parking area to get to the best in tent camping at Horseshoe, and some of the best in West Virginia. Leave your car parked by the big field and enter a much more wooded and less groomed area (read: natural) than the main campground. White pine, birch, and an understory of hemlock and rhododendron are your campsite borders. These 12 walk-in sites assure you an RV-free zone. Follow a path that leads past two campsites under tall trees next to a hill. Most of the remaining tent campsites lie along Horseshoe Run in one good setting after another. Between the tent camper's area and the big field are the bathrooms for tent campers. Water spigots are located here and in the main campground.

By now you have noticed Horseshoe Run. There is a nice swimming hole here by the field. It's a great place to cool off. Trout fishermen will want to get a little bit away from the swimming hole to vie for trout in Horseshoe Run. If you want to try another watery experience, canoe the Cheat River. Nearby is the Blackwater Outdoor Center. They will provide canoes and shuttle for a fee on a 35-mile stretch of paddle-able river. Pick the length of your trip. You can reach them at (304) 478-4456 or www. raftboc.com. The bass fishing in the Cheat is said to be good.

Trails leave the campground if you want to hike. The Two Camp Trail (Forest Trail #111) leaves the campground near the pay station. It heads downstream for a level 0.4 mile before intersecting the Losh Trail (Forest Trail #155). Take the Losh Trail across Horseshoe Run on a footbridge to climb 1.8 miles to a trail shelter in the high country. Turn on the Dorman Ridge Trail (Forest Trail #153) for a ramble through open areas with mountain panoramas. Return the way you came.

Up McKinley Run, the side stream by the main campground, is another footpath (Forest Trail #154) that climbs along its namesake stream toward Close Mountain. If you want to see some waterfalls, try the Maxwell Run Trail (Forest Trail #157). It starts about a mile back down the road toward Parsons and climbs 2 miles up Maxwell Run in a narrow valley. Return the way you came. And after you come to Horseshoe Run Campground, odds are you will return.

To get there: From Parsons, drive north on WV 72 for 6 miles to the Cheat River Bridge at St. George. There is a sign for Horseshoe Campground here. Cross the Cheat River and enter St. George. Soon turn right on Holly Meadows Road (Route 1) and follow it for 3 miles to Horseshoe Run Road (Route 7). Turn left on Horseshoe Run Road and follow it for 3.3 miles to Horseshoe Campground, which will be on your left.

KEY INFORMATION

Horseshoe Run Campground
P.O. Box 368
Parsons, WV 26287

Operated by: U.S. Forest Service

Information: (304) 478-3251, reservations (877) 444-6777, www.fs.fed.us/r9/mon/

Open: May 5 through November 31

Individual sites: 25

Each site has: Main Loop: picnic table, fire grate, tent pad, lantern post; Tent Camper's Area: picnic table, stand-up grill, fire grate

Site assignment: Reservations accepted, but not required

Registration: By phone, or self-registration at campground

Facilities: Water spigots, vault toilets

Parking: At campsites only for Main Loop or tent camper's parking area

Fee: $7 per night

Elevation: 1,750 feet

Restrictions
 Pets—On leash only
 Fires—In fire grates only
 Alcoholic beverages—At campsites only
 Vehicles—None
 Other—14-day stay limit

ISLAND

Bartow

Island Campground, located on an island of the East Fork Greenbrier River, is small and rustic. Since it is open year-round, it can be a destination on milder days during the cooler months. Hikers and anglers enjoy the little-used gem of the East Fork Trail, which starts at the campground. Other natural nearby attractions are Lake Buffalo, also with hiking and fishing opportunities, and Gaudineer Scenic Area, which features an old-growth spruce stand. The Civil War–era Cheat Summit Fort also merits a visit.

Pull off West Virginia 28 and travel the gravel road to Island Campground. You will first notice the vault toilets off to your right. This is also the commencement of the East Fork Trail. Immediately to your left is a gravel road leading 50 yards to an isolated campsite in a stand of hemlocks that offers maximum privacy, even though it is the closest to WV 28. Autos will be slightly audible over the babbling of East Fork Greenbrier River.

Continue forward and cross a wood bridge over a small streamlet. To your left lies a somewhat shaded campsite beside the watercourse. This site is a little on the small side but has no other campsites nearby. Cross a second little wood bridge over another wet meander. To your left is another campsite shaded by hemlocks and open to the stream beside it. This site has ade-

CAMPGROUND RATINGS

Beauty: ★★★

Site privacy: ★★★★

Site spaciousness: ★★★★

Quiet: ★★★

Security: ★★★

Cleanliness/upkeep: ★★★

This quiet getaway is open year-round and boasts a variety of nearby forest attractions.

ALLEGHENY HIGHLANDS

quate size and much privacy.

Finally, come to an auto turnaround with three campsites spoking off. The first site on the right is the largest. It is encircled by trees and fairly near the East Fork. Next, an old road runs straight to the creek where there was once a bridge. An excellent ultra-shaded tent area hunkers beside this, down in a flat. Hemlocks crowd the sky overhead, and the East Fork is just a few steps away. Tent campers here will be sung to sleep by the stream.

The final campsite is level and well-shaded, if short on room. Since the campground as a whole is short on sites, most folks pass Island Campground by for the bigger, more publicized campgrounds around. However, it has been a traditional camping ground for decades and will fill only on summer holidays and a few great weather weekends.

Island Campground makes a fine base camp for exploring the East Fork Greenbrier Valley. The East Fork Trail runs along this stream and has proven a pleasure in any season. Spring brings wildflowers aplenty. In summer, anglers vie for trout or cool off in swimming holes. Fall's paintbrush warms the valley with vibrant colors, and in winter the lack of mandatory fords makes this a viable hike. However, take care during higher flows.

Lake Buffalo, which you passed on the way to Island from Bartow, is 20 acres of aquatic beauty. The clear water, set in a mountain valley, offers fishing for trout, bass, and bream. There is a trail around the lake commonly used by anglers and hikers.

On U.S. 250 beyond Bartow is the Gaudineer Scenic Area where one hundred forty acres of forest land have been set aside thanks to their exceptional beauty.

Fifty of these acres are completely virgin woods—primarily red spruce. Some red spruce exceed three feet in diameter and are over 300 years old! You'll also find yellow birch, beech, and maple.

A short distance beyond Gaudineer Scenic Area lies Cheat Summit Fort. This Union Fort was built in 1861 to protect the Staunton-Parkersburg Turnpike. Confederates and Yankees skirmished in the region. This was allegedly the site where the telegraph was first used during the Civil War. There are good views from the ridge here, and you will find Fort Milroy Cemetery nearby. Also of note is the nearby Strip Mine Trail, which offers more views and insight into West Virginia strip mining culture. To get to this area turn left from U.S. 250 near Cheat Bridge, turn right at the T junction, and go 1 mile to the top of the ridge. Enjoy.

To get there: From Bartow, at the intersection of U.S. 250 and WV 28/92, head north on WV 28/U.S. 250 for 2.2 miles. As U.S. 250 veers right, continue on WV 28 for 2.6 miles. Island Campground will be on your left.

KEY INFORMATION

Island Campground
Box 67
Bartow, WV 24920

Operated by: U.S. Forest Service

Information: (304) 456-3335, www.fs.fed.us/r9/mon/

Open: Year-round

Individual sites: 6

Each site has: Picnic table, fire grate, lantern post

Site assignment: First come, first served; no reservations

Registration: No registration

Facilities: Vault toilets; (bring water)

Parking: At campsites only

Fee: None

Elevation: 2,600 feet

Restrictions

Pets—On leash only

Fires—In fire grates only

Alcoholic beverages—At campsites only

Vehicles—None

Other—14-day stay limit

KUMBRABOW STATE FOREST

Huttonsville

This forest is in the high country. In fact, it is West Virginia's highest state forest, with elevations ranging from 3,000 to 3,855 feet. Its forest is northern hardwoods: cherry and yellow birch. Before the state acquired Kumbrabow, the mountains here were logged for the immense stands of spruce and hemlock. The forest has since recovered to become one of the most attractive, least-used forests in the entire state. I surmise that limited access and lack of knowledge lead to the absence of campers. But now you have no excuse not to have a great tent-camping experience here.

The Mill Creek Camping Area is set alongside Mill Creek, which native brook trout call home. Mill Creek is off to your left, with a smaller creek coming in to your right. Descend among rhododendron, passing a water pump. Notice the first seven campsites also have stone fireplaces in addition to the fire grates. These are leftovers from the handiwork of the Civilian Conservation Corps, who built this original camping area. The sites are medium to small, but very scenic, especially if you like camping on a tumbling stream.

Cross a low-water bridge over Mill Creek and come to the "newer" camping area. A short road to your left leads to two streamside campsites. The main road passes between a field and the stream. These streamside campsites are larger, with rhododendron providing camp site barriers.

CAMPGROUND RATINGS

Beauty: ★★★★
Site privacy: ★★★
Site spaciousness: ★★★
Quiet: ★★★★★
Security: ★★★★★
Cleanliness/upkeep: ★★★★

This is the state's most under-utilized natural resource.

ALLEGHENY HIGHLANDS

Large stones also make for campsite barriers. Pass a disabled-accessible campsite and a second water pump. A few more campsites are strung along Mill Creek. I would stay at any of these campsites—they are all good.

You can get a campsite here anytime, barring summer holidays. Be apprised that the shoulder seasons can be chilly. Snow can fall in April, and generally any night will be cool—perfect for that evening campfire—at this extremely rural, rustic getaway that is like a trip back in time.

The forest covers 9,474 acres of rugged mountain land, where the bears roam and the native trout swim free. The primary attraction of Kumbrabow is angling for the native brookies along Mill Creek and its tributaries. Tributaries such as Meatbox Run and Potato Hole Run are not as productive as Mill Creek, but provide the angler with a scenic experience even if the fish aren't biting.

If you like hiking in solitude, come here. Chances are you won't see another person, but you may see some wildlife. The Rich Mountain Fire Trail follows the northern border of the forest and takes you to the highest point in the area, Buck Knob. Several connector paths drop off from Rich Mountain. The Raven Rocks Trail drops sharply from the Rich Mountain Fire Tower trail to a rock overlook. You can use the Potato Hole and the Meatbox Run Trails for a loop.

From the camping area, follow the Mill Creek Trail down past the forest cabins and come to Mill Creek Falls. This path can also be used for fishing access. The Mill Ridge trails are on the far side of Mill Creek. There are loop opportunities here, using the Mill Ridge, Clay Run, and Mowery Paths.

Also on forest grounds is the old Camp Bowers. This is an old CCC camp that was occupied from 1934 to 1941. You can see remains of where the young men lived while developing Kumbrabow. By the way, Kumbrabow is not an Indian name. It is the agglomeration of three names of families, KUMp-BRAdy-BOWers, who helped in the acquisition of the forest land.

A nearby attraction is the hamlet of Helvetia. It is a community of Swiss descendants who originally settled there in the 1860s. They have preserved many Swiss traditions. There is an historic district in the town. To get there, pass the forest office, then turn right on Turkeybone Road (County Road 45) and make a scenic drive to Helvetia. The Swiss were right to settle in this high, mountainous section of West Virginia.

To get there: From Huttonsville, drive south on U.S. 219 for 7 miles to Kumbrabow Road (CR 216). There will be a sign for the state forest here. Turn right on CR 216 and follow the gravel road 5 miles into the state forest.

KEY INFORMATION

Kumbrabow State Forest
Box 65
Huttonsville, WV 26273

Operated by: West Virginia State Parks

Information: (304) 335-2219, www.wvparks.com/kumbrabow

Open: Mid-April through mid-December

Individual sites: 13

Each site has: Picnic table, fire grate

Site assignment: First come first served; no reservations

Registration: At park office or ranger will come by to register you

Facilities: Vault toilet, pump well

Parking: At campsites only

Fee: $7 per night

Elevation: 3,000 feet

Restrictions:

Pets—On leash only

Fires—In fire grates only

Alcoholic beverages—Prohibited

Vehicles—None

Other—14-day stay limit

LAKE SHERWOOD

Neola

West Virginia has many pretty valleys bordered by high mountains. That describes much of the state. However, you just may agree with me that the valley of Meadow Creek, bordered by Meadow Creek Mountain on one side and the state-line range of the Alleghenies on the other, may be the Mountain State's prettiest valley. Meadow Creek was dammed in 1958, and Lake Sherwood was born. This capped off the scenery.

Lake Sherwood Recreation Area is very well kept, maintaining its attractiveness. The developments did nothing to spoil the natural allure; the developments are the means by which you can indulge in the area's resources. Swimming, fishing, hiking, and all-around relaxing are on the agenda when you find yourself at the terminus of Lake Sherwood Road.

As you drive up, Lake Sherwood will be on your right. The swim beaches and main boat landing are over that way, too. Then come to the year-round camping area, West Shore Loop. The forest is dominated by white pine, oak, and hickory, with a lot of dogwood. Wooden posts delineate the campsites. Several campsites overlook the lake from a bluff. This loop has a full bathhouse for summer and vault toilets and pump well for the off season. The sites are very spacious, which adds to the campsite privacy. Some campers pull their boats right up to the shore from the lake.

CAMPGROUND RATINGS

Beauty:	★★★★★
Site privacy:	★★★★
Site spaciousness:	★★★★
Quiet:	★★★★
Security:	★★★★★
Cleanliness/upkeep:	★★★★★

There is plenty to do here at this recreation area, situated on West Virginia's prettiest lake.

ALLEGHENY HIGHLANDS

The Pine Run Loop is on a little higher and drier land. It is heavier on Virginia pine and has a more open forest, but is still very pretty. The main loop here swings out toward the lake and has several sites that overlook the reservoir. There is another spur road on the far side of a rill that has very large campsites that can be reserved. At the end of this road is another boat launch.

The final loop, Meadow Creek, is also in a pine-oak-hickory complex. All 35 sites can be reserved here. The camp-

sites are so well designed, well spaced out, and big that they attract some RVs. Just grin and bear it here; this place is worth it. The spur road with another boat launch has some campsites very close to the lake. The loop turns away from the lake, climbs a hill, and splits. There are more good campsites on both roads.

Campground hosts are at all the loops, making their contribution, giving Lake Sherwood that well-cared-for look. Water spigots are spread through all the loops, as are bathhouses. If you are coming from far away, reserve a campsite. Lake Sherwood deservedly fills on all major holidays and many weekends. It stays busy during the week in high summer. Autumn is an excellent alternative time with the fall colors reflecting off the lake.

The 144-acre impoundment lures anglers in for some potentially exciting fishing. Tiger muskie, a large predatory fish, are stocked here. They can run 15 pounds or more. Largemouth bass, bluegill, and catfish round out the platter. Artificial fish-attracting reefs have been put in the lake. For the peace of all lake visitors, only electric motors are allowed.

Boats and canoes are available for rent near the main boat launch. Also near the launch are two beaches and a bathhouse. One beach is on the main shore;

the other is on an island accessible by a wooden bridge. The swimming area is between the two beaches. You will rarely find a more attractive setting to cool off.

Several trails leave directly from the recreation area. The most notable is the Lake Sherwood Trail. It makes a 3.2-mile loop around the lake. This is a moderate walk suitable for the entire family. The Virginia Trail spurs off the Lake Sherwood Trail and heads 0.6 mile up to the Allegheny Mountain Trail. From here, you walk the state-line ridge for 3.6 miles and gain views of Lake Sherwood and Lake Moomow in Virginia.

The Meadow Creek Trail starts at the head of Lake Sherwood and parallels Meadow Creek, crossing the stream several times amid thickets of rhododendron, intersecting the Connector Trail at 2.7 miles. Here, you can turn right and make a 10-mile loop back to the Meadow Creek bridge at Lake Sherwood using the Allegheny Mountain and Lake Sherwood Trails. This is one of West Virginia's finest circuit hikes.

Bikers can pedal the recreation area roads or head a mile up the Upper Meadow Trail to tackle the Meadow Creek Mountain. This old road runs along the crest of the ridge, offering scenic views into Lake Sherwood. You can continue north for 3-plus miles to intersect the Connector Trail for more loop possibilities. Another possibility is lying around your campsite taking in the scenery at West Virginia's prettiest lake. Come here and rate it for yourself.

To get there: From Exit 181 on I-64 at White Sulpher Springs, drive 15 miles north on WV 92 to Neola. From Neola, travel east on Lake Sherwood Road for 11 miles and enter the recreation area.

KEY INFORMATION

Lake Sherwood
410 East Main Street
White Sulphur Springs, WV
24986

Operated by: U.S. Forest Service

Information: (304) 536-2144, reservations (877) 444-6777, www.fs.fed.us/r9/mon/

Open: West Shore: year-round; rest of campground: mid-May through early September

Individual sites: 95

Each site has: Picnic table, fire grate, lantern post, tent pad

Site assignment: Reservations accepted, but not required

Registration: By phone, or at campground entrance kiosk

Facilities: Hot showers, flush toilets, water spigots

Parking: At campsites only

Fee: $12 per night

Elevation: 2,670 feet

Restrictions:

Pets—On leash only

Fires—In fire grates only

Alcoholic beverages—At campsites only

Vehicles—None

Other—14-day stay limit

LAUREL FORK

Glady

This large, pretty, and free campground is situated between two of Monongahela National Forest's premier wilderness areas, Laurel Fork North and Laurel Fork South. Come here and plan to do a little exploring. And when you return to your campsite, you can enjoy ridgetop views and a relaxing place to contemplate the natural surroundings, for that is one key element of tent camping.

Drop from Forest Road 14 into the Laurel Fork Valley. Come to a cleared area with forest buildings on your left. The forest service used this location as wildlife management headquarters, but the buildings are now unoccupied. Originally this was a Civilian Conservation Corps Camp. You, however, can enjoy the area as a campground.

Turn right into the upper loop. This loop is huge for so few campsites. Attractive wood fences protect clear areas. Pass the pump well and come to a good campsite on your left, which lies between a row of Norway spruce trees and Laurel Fork. The loop splits right into a clearing dotted with a few trees. Three campsites are out in the open here. They offer the maximum in spaciousness and have good views, but no shade.

The fourth site is banked against the woods and has good views and afternoon shade. A pair of vault toilets are nearby, and beyond them is a great campsite beneath a grove of red pine. This shady site is adjacent to the Laurel River south trailhead.

CAMPGROUND RATINGS

Beauty:	★★★★
Site privacy:	★★★
Site spaciousness:	★★★★★
Quiet:	★★★★★
Security:	★★★
Cleanliness/upkeep:	★★★★

Laurel Fork lies between two scenic wilderness areas.

ALLEGHENY HIGHLANDS

The loop swings around along Laurel Creek and passes two large sites that are directly on the creek and have good morning shade. There is also one campsite in the open middle of the loop.

Return to the main road and cross Laurel Fork on a wood bridge. Immediately to your right is a well-shaded popular campsite that is by itself along the river. Enter the lower loop, which is also oversized, as are the campsites. The center of the loop is grassy and has a covered picnic shelter in it. This large central clearing allows mountain views for all campers. More wood fences delineate the camping areas.

Pass a vault toilet on your right, then come to the first campsite. It benefits from shady spruce and pine trees. This campsite is right next to the trail that enters the Laurel Fork North Wilderness. Just on the other side of the trailhead is a campsite that has good views and a good mixture of sun and shade provided by spruce and hawthorn trees. Then there is a more open site right next to Laurel Fork that is coveted by campers. An open campsite by the water precedes a very large one that has it all: sun, shade, and river access.

The campsites here may be the largest in all the state. The setting is very pretty, but the price paid for the views is a lack of privacy. The small number of campsites makes up for the lack of privacy. Expect Laurel Fork Campground to fill on summer holidays and some weekends. Try to come during the week in summer. A great time to visit is in autumn.

Campers here are of two stripes: those who like to explore and those who like to relax. Active campers have two trails leaving right from the campground into the wilderness areas. Technically, they are both the Laurel River

Trail, but one heads into Laurel Fork Wilderness North and the other into Laurel Fork Wilderness South. After you take a hike, you will understand why these scenic areas were protected as federally designated wildernesses totaling nearly 12,000 acres.

Take the Laurel River Trail from the upper loop and head upstream along Laurel Fork, passing some attractive woods carpeted in ferns. Numerous meadows add to the scenery. Beaver evidence is everywhere, and you may even see one of these industrious critters. A good destination is the confluence of Camp Five Run and Laurel Fork, 4 miles distant. Here is a large meadow and a shady evergreen thicket, where you can sprawl out in the sun or have a picnic in the shade. The Laurel River Trail also leaves the lower loop and passes many fields. The creek is bigger here and offers angling opportunities. It heads down several miles in an ever-widening valley. Be advised these wilderness trails are not as well marked as most national forest paths.

I hiked both trails. As an active camper I explored the wilderness areas, then joined the other Laurel Fork camper types, the relaxers, and stretched out on a hammock. It felt good to take in the scenery and enjoy another evening of tent camping in the Mountain State.

To get there: From the post office in Glady, drive east on FS 422 for 4.6 miles to FS 14. Drive south on FS 14 for 0.3 mile to FS 423. Turn left on FS 423 and drive 1.5 miles down to Laurel Fork Campground.

KEY INFORMATION

Laurel Fork Campground
Box 67
Bartow, WV 24920

Operated by: U.S. Forest Service

Information: (304) 456-3335, www.fs.fed.us/r9/mon/

Open: Year-round

Individual sites: 14

Each site has: Picnic table, fire ring, lantern post, waste can

Site assignment: First come, first served; no reservations

Registration: No registration

Facilities: Vault toilet, pump well (available May–November)

Parking: At campsites only

Fee: None

Elevation: 3,100 feet

Restrictions

Pets—On leash only

Fires—In fire rings only

Alcoholic beverages—At campsites only

Vehicles—None

Other—14-day stay limit

POCAHONTAS

Marlinton

Pocahontas is a great destination in many ways: it is an extremely pretty campground set in a forest of giant white pine beside a valley stream; it is little used, inexpensive, and has quiet, yet well-maintained, mountain biking and hiking trails leaving directly from the campground. So why the unpopularity? The campground is a little too close to West Virginia 92. WV 92 is not heavily traveled, but you can hear every car that passes by. If you can't overlook this fact, then read no further.

I was skeptical about Pocahontas myself, until I gave it a try. It was raining when I arrived, so I set up the tent, then fell asleep to the raindrops on the tent fly. Around 4 p.m. I awoke, and the rain had stopped, though the skies were still cloudy. After powering down some coffee, I took off up the Two Lick Run Trail, taking in the tranquil scenery. Later that night I sat beside the campfire, feeling sorry for all those passing by Pocahontas in their cars. By the way, it was a Friday night and I had the campground all to myself.

Pocahontas Campground is set in a wooded flat along Cochran Creek. Leave WV 92 and pass the Two Lick Run trailhead and come to the pump well. Some pump wells have funny-tasting water, especially right after it first comes out, but this pump puts out nothing but pure sweet water. And I've drunk a lot of pump-well water in my camping days. This is some

CAMPGROUND RATINGS

Beauty:	★★★★★
Site privacy:	★★★
Site spaciousness:	★★★★
Quiet:	★★★
Security:	★★★
Cleanliness/upkeep:	★★★★

Pocahontas is often overlooked because of other nearby recreation sites. Mountain bikers will be especially pleased with this place.

ALLEGHENY HIGHLANDS

of the finest water I've ever drunk.

The first campsite is across from the sweetwater pump well. You'll notice the forest overhead: there are huge white pines above an understory of maple, musclewood, hemlock, and a few oaks. Smaller trees thicken the understory. Then come to two more large campsites with a lot of privacy. Unfortunately, these are the closest to the road.

Swing around and more towering pines rise overhead. Large, isolated campsites are on the outside of the loop. Pass a small rill that meanders through the center of the loop. Now the oval parallels Cochran Creek. The forest is thicker, with more hemlock trees and some rhododendron. The last few sites either border Cochran Creek or the small campground rill. Two vault toilets, one for each gender, complete the campground.

I believe you can get a campsite here just about any day it is open. I am all for leaving the sounds of civilization behind, but the advantages of Pocahontas simply outweigh the disadvantages. It seemed I had my own private recreation area. No one was on the trails, hiking or biking. And this was in mid-May.

Mountain bikers especially shouldn't miss Pocahontas. Two loops marked for the pedaling set leave directly from the campground. The Middle Mountain Route leaves the campground and goes left on WV 92 to Forest Road 790. Climb FS 790, a gated road, to Forest Road 962. Travel 6 miles north to the Middle Mountain Trail for some single-track action, then on down to West Virginia 39, then right again on WV 92 for a 13-mile loop. The Lockridge Mountain Route is a little easier. Turn right out of the campground on WV 92, then right on WV 39 for 0.5 mile. Turn left on Forest Road 55, then start your return on the gated Forest Road 345 and circle back via Rimel Picnic Area. This is a 13-mile loop, too. These marked bike routes are explained on a kiosk at the campground.

Hikers and bikers can enjoy the Two Lick Run Trail that starts at the front of the campground. It is a 4.6-mile pathway that climbs up Middle Mountain and swings around the head of the Two Lick watershed to make a loop. A shorter 1.8-mile loop uses the Two Lick Bottom Trail and part of the Two Lick Run Trail.

The nearby Laurel Creek Trail leaves Rimel Picnic Area, back on WV 39. The trail follows an old railroad grade to climb up and reach a backpacker's shelter at 5 miles, then circles around the slopes of Lockridge Mountain, returning to the picnic area at mile 8.

Supplies can be had back in Marlinton. It is but 4 miles to the mineral springs at Minnehaha. Pocahontas is one place where you shouldn't let an occasional passing car ruin your tent-camping experience.

To get there: From Marlinton, drive east on WV 39/92 for 13 miles to where WV 92 splits off to the right. Turn right on WV 92 south and follow it for 2 miles to Pocahontas Recreation Area, which will be on your left.

KEY INFORMATION

Pocahontas
P.O. Box 210
Marlinton, WV 24954-0210

Operated by: U.S. Forest Service

Information: (304) 799-4334, www.fs.fed.us/r9/mon/

Open: March 15 through December 15

Individual sites: 8

Each site has: Picnic table, fire grate, lantern post

Site assignment: First come, first served; no reservations

Registration: Self-registration on site

Facilities: Pump well, vault toilets

Parking: At campsites only

Fee: $6 per night

Elevation: 2,490 feet

Restrictions:

 Pets—On leash only

 Fires—In fire grates only

 Alcoholic beverages—At camp-sites only

 Vehicles—None

 Other—14-day stay limit

SENECA STATE FOREST

Dunmore

Seneca is West Virginia's oldest state forest. It is also one of its quietest. Long ago, the Seneca Indians roamed the area—that's how the forest received its name. Now, you can traverse the very hills and hollows that the Seneca walked and enjoy some more recent history at Cass Scenic Railroad State Park. Re-enter the modern era with a visit to the National Radio Observatory in nearby Green Bank. Finally, return to the small campground set in a handsome hollow. No doubt, it is an odd collection of attractions in the area, but it allows you to appreciate the evolution of West Virginia through the generations.

You will also appreciate this campground. A Seneca ranger claims it is the finest in the state. He has a case. The campground is set along a pair of small mountain streams. Rhododendron crowds the creeks. Overhead, a mixed forest of white pine, hemlock, maple, and some oak shade the campsites. Steep hills stretch high around you.

The campsites are sheltered among the rhododendron away from the road. Camping areas have been leveled and set far apart from one another. Little bridges lead over the streams to most campsites, adding a certain quaintness to the natural beauty. Some campsites are heavily shaded by hemlock. Pass a vault toilet as you head toward the main hollow. Then the road splits up two small hollows. To the left is a

CAMPGROUND RATINGS

Beauty:	★★★★★
Site privacy:	★★★★
Site spaciousness:	★★★★★
Quiet:	★★★★
Security:	★★★★
Cleanliness/upkeep:	★★★★★

You will love the campground at West Virginia's oldest state forest.

ALLEGHENY HIGHLANDS

road leading to two campsites. A grassy area lies between where the road splits. Here is the hand-pump well and two more vault toilets. Heavy rhododendron lies by the campsites along the creek. The road ends at a very private campsite. The Great Laurel Trail starts here.

The other road heads up the right-hand hollow. There are two more very private and secluded campsites that are the best in tent camping. This neat-as-a-pin, well-groomed campground has ten sites; it could hold 20. However, even with its small numbers, it very rarely—if ever—fills, making for a relaxing experience from the time you strike up your tent until you store it away in the trunk. Also of note is the coin-operated shower. This amenity is available behind the park office.

Trails for hikers and bikers lace the state forest. The Horseshoe Trail leaves the campground and makes a 1.5-mile loop. The Great Rhododendron Trail, named after the West Virginia state flower, leads a half mile from the campground to connect to the Hilltop Trail, one among many other paths around. The long-running Allegheny Trail meanders through the forest and has a trail shelter for overnight campers. The Fire Tower Trail leads to great views.

Many trails and back roads are open to mountain bikers. The Loop Road leads up toward the fire tower and past the shelter along the Allegheny Trail. Just 5 miles away is the Greenbrier River Trail, a long-distance rail trail that parallels the Greenbrier River, where there are also angling opportunities. On park property you can fish four-acre Seneca Lake. It has trout, bass, and bluegill in its clear waters.

A West Virginia State Park highlight is the Cass Scenic Railroad, built in 1902. The train, authentic locomotives with logging flatcars made into passenger coaches, leaves the restored town of Cass and climbs up the mountains to open fields and, later, to Whitaker Station. Then you can head up to Bald Knob, the second-highest point in the state at 4,842 feet. There are great views from the overlook here. To reach Cass, leave north on WV 28 at the campground and follow the signs.

Also of interest is the National Radio Astronomy Observatory. It has been the focal point of radio astronomy for decades. Daily guided tours are offered Memorial Day through Labor Day. You can see science at work and learn more about how we learn about the world beyond our world. Self-guided walking and bicycling tours of the observatory can be taken any time of year. Head north on WV 28 from the campground and follow the signs to the observatory near Cass. After touring the observatory, you can enjoy your down-to-earth campground at Seneca State Forest.

To get there: From Marlinton, drive east on WV 39 for 5 miles to WV 28. Turn left on WV 28 and follow it 11 miles north to Seneca State Forest.

KEY INFORMATION

Seneca State Forest
Route 1, Box 140
Dunmore, WV 24934

Operated by: West Virginia State Parks

Information: (304) 799-6213, www.wvparks.com/seneca

Open: Mid-April through early December

Individual sites: 10

Each site has: Picnic table, fire grate, tent pad

Site assignment: First come, first served; no reservation

Registration: Self-registration on site

Facilities: Coin-operated shower, vault toilet, hand-pump well

Parking: At campsites only

Fee: $7 per night

Elevation: 2,600 feet

Restrictions:

Pets—On leash only

Fires—In fire grates only

Alcoholic beverages—Prohibited

Vehicles—Two vehicles per site

Other—14-day stay limit

SPRUCE KNOB LAKE

Seneca Rocks

Spruce Knob is a component of the Spruce Knob–Seneca Rocks National Recreation Area. This is the land of superlatives: the highest campground in the state, the highest lake in the state, and the highest point in the state. The surrounding mountains are laced with trails that traverse the forests, fields, and streams. Campers can enjoy the cool air of the high country at drive-up campsites or walk-in tent campsites.

No matter where your point of entry is, it is a good drive through rugged terrain to reach the campground. Bring all supplies you will need. Enter the paved campground loop and drive uphill through a northern hardwood forest. This deciduous woodland, perched at 4,000 feet, will be one of the last places to leaf out and one of the first places to turn colorful in the state.

Begin to pass campsites tucked away in deep woods off the loop road. The understory is thick here, which is good for campsite privacy. The campsites are average in size. There are numerous combinations of sun and shade here, though most campsites are on the shady side.

The hill you climb is pretty steep, but the campsites have been leveled. This vertical variation adds beauty and privacy to already secluded campsites. The hill tops out at campsite #20. More attractive campsites are spread out along both sides of the

CAMPGROUND RATINGS

Beauty:	★★★★
Site privacy:	★★★★
Site spaciousness:	★★★
Quiet:	★★★★★
Security:	★★★
Cleanliness/upkeep:	★★★★

The highest campground in this guidebook lies near the highest point in the state.

ALLEGHENY HIGHLANDS

road as it heads back down the mountainside.

Make a sharp left turn and the campground road runs perpendicular to the slope of the mountain. Along here are many walk-in sites that will appeal to tent campers. Wooden steps lead up or down to the spots that are just a short walk into the woods. Campers park parallel to the loop road.

Vault toilets and pump wells are spread throughout the campground. There is a solar-powered well near camp-site #20 that delivers water

through a spigot. Spruce Knob Lake will fill on summer holidays, but is not busy during spring, which can be cool, and after August, when the campground will be its most attractive, draped in fall's decorations. Freezing temperatures are a real possibility during the shoulder seasons.

You must check out the area's superlatives. First, make the short drive to the actual Spruce Knob. This is West Virginia's highest point, at 4,861 feet. The Whispering Spruce Trail encircles the observation tower, going through highland woods to open up on a rocky field with great views. Farther-reaching 360-degree views can be had from the tower.

Spruce Knob Lake is an attractive impoundment and offers good views from the water looking toward Spruce Knob. No gas motors are allowed on the 25-acre lake. Take your self-propelled boat to angle for rainbow trout and some bass. Bank fishermen can use the 1-mile trail that encircles the lake. This walk is a pleasure for anyone, whether you fish or not. The Gatewood Trail makes a 2-mile loop and is connected to the campground by the Short Trail.

Hikers will also be interested in the Seneca Creek Backcountry. This primitive area lies just north of Forest Road 1 near the campground. There are streams and meadows and views in the area. The most popular hike is the 5-mile trek to Upper Seneca Falls on the Seneca Creek Trail. The Allegheny Mountain Trail follows the backbone ridge of the area. The Lumberjack Trail leads out to the High Meadows Trail, where there are great views. All in all, 70 miles of paths traverse this country. The national forest produces a good handout of the Seneca Creek Backcountry that should keep you more than busy during your stay at Spruce Knob Lake.

To get there: From Seneca Rocks, drive south for 10 miles to the hamlet of Cherry Grove and WV 28. Turn right on WV 28 and follow it for 3 miles to Sawmill Run Road (CR 28/10). Turn right on Sawmill Run Road and follow it for 8.4 miles to FS 112. Turn right on FS 112 and follow it for 0.6 mile to FS 1. Turn left on FS 1 and follow it for 0.6 mile to Spruce Knob Lake Campground, which will be on your right.

KEY INFORMATION

Spruce Knob Lake Campground
HC 59, Box 240
Petersburg, WV 26847

Operated by: U.S. Forest Service

Information: (304) 257-4488, www.fs.fed.us/r9/mon/

Open: Mid-April through December

Individual sites: 30 drive-up sites, 12 walk-in tent sites

Each site has: Picnic table, fire grate, lantern post, tent pad

Site assignment: First come, first served; no reservations

Registration: Self-registration on site

Facilities: Vault toilets, pump well, solar water spigot

Parking: At campsites and walk-in parking area

Fee: $7 per night drive-up sites, $5 per night walk-in tent sites

Elevation: 4,000 feet

Restrictions:

   Pets—On leash only

   Fires—In fire grates only

   Alcoholic beverages—At campsites only

   Vehicles—None

   Other—14-day stay limit

SUMMIT LAKE

Richwood

Summit Lake is an example of a well-developed recreation area, not as in overly developed, but developed to the point of making the area more user friendly. The two forks of Coats Run once quietly dropped down to the North Fork Cherry River. Now they feed the impoundment of Summit Lake, which rests in a flat high above the North Fork Cherry River. A scenic hiking trail lies around Summit Lake, which is stocked for fishing. Other pathways comb the area and lead to the primitive Cranberry Backcountry, where there are more hiking, fishing, and nature study opportunities. Beyond this lies still more Monongahela National Forest pursuits.

The name Summit Lake seems appropriate after the drive up from Richwood. Turn onto the paved campground road, pass the fee station, and enter the first of two loops. This loop has nine campsites, tiered and leveled into a mountainside.

Seven of the nine campsites are on the inside of the loop. Each campsite pull-in is paved. Each graveled area houses a picnic table, fire grate, and lantern post. The pebbles are a little tough to drive a tent stake into. Overhead are deciduous trees, such as tulip trees, sugar maples, beech, and oaks. A set of vault toilets and a water spigot lie on the outside of the loop. A trail heads to Summit Lake from near the toilets.

CAMPGROUND RATINGS

Beauty:	★★★
Site privacy:	★★★★
Site spaciousness:	★★★
Quiet:	★★★★
Security:	★★★
Cleanliness/upkeep:	★★★★

Summit Lake offers water recreation in the southwest Monongahela National Forest.

ALLEGHENY HIGHLANDS

The second loop, also paved, is farther up the main road. Twenty-four well-spaced campsites make this a much bigger loop. The campsites, mostly on the outside of the loop with nice views into the surrounding woods, are also cut into the mountainside and leveled. Some of the campsites are pull through. Others have the picnic tables and camping areas just into the woods for added privacy.

There are two pump wells on this loop, but the water I got tasted rusty. Get your

water from the spigot at the first loop. There are two sets of vault toilets for each gender here. A foot trail leaves near the first set of bathrooms for Summit Lake.

And Summit Lake is the center of the action around here—it is 42 acres of mountain-rimmed clarity. Beneath the surface swim all manner of fish: brook trout, brown trout, rainbow trout, largemouth bass, and crappie. Anglers can fish from the shore or get out on a boat. Electric motors and arm power are the only means of advancing your craft over the lake. Most bank fishermen like to toss their line in from the dam. There is also an all-access dock near the boat launch.

The scenic aspects of the lake can be best appreciated from the Summit Lake Trail. Start your hike near the boat put-in by an aspen tree, head north, and step over the two lake feeder streams. Turn back south and complete your 1.8-mile loop by crossing over the dam.

The second best hike in the area is the Fisherman's Trail. This starts near the campground at the end of Forest Road 77. FS 77 starts just across from the turn into the campground. Drive the mile or so to the gate on FS 77 and come to a trailhead. To your left heading straight down is the Fisherman's Trail (#231). This immediately drops down along Pleasant Hollow, arriving on the Cranberry River and a trail shelter in 1.5 miles. Here, you can hike and fish in either direction in the Cranberry Backcountry. There are 26,000 acres and over 60 miles of trails to enjoy in this primitive area.

Also at the end of FS 77 is the Pocahontas Trail (#263). To your left up a hill, it is 1.6 miles to Hanging Rock. You can return by the gated Forest Road 99. To your right it is 5 miles to Mikes Knob. There, the Pocahontas Trail connects to the end of gated FS 77 to the top of the mountain where a fire tower once stood. Mountain bikers should note that FS 99 and FS 77 make excellent rides, as do many other forest roads in the area. A map of the Monongahela National Forest really helps here.

For folks in cars, the best ride is the Highland Scenic Highway, a.k.a. West Virginia 39/55. You drove a portion of the road from Richwood. Continue the drive up to Cranberry Visitor Center (worth a stop), then turn left on West Virginia 150, which is the continuation of the scenic highway. Along the way are many overlooks. Two trails of note here are the High Rocks Trail, which has a great view, and the Black Mountain Loop, which has views, solitude, and history.

To get there: From Richwood, drive east on WV 39/55 for 7.2 miles to Summit Lake Road (CR 39/5). Turn left on Summit Lake Road and climb for 2.1 miles to Summit Lake Campground.

KEY INFORMATION

Summit Lake Campground
Box 110
Richwood, WV 26261

Operated by: U.S. Forest Service

Information: (304) 846-2695; www.fs.fed.us/r9/mon/

Open: March 15 through November 30

Individual sites: 33

Each site has: Picnic table, fire grate, lantern post

Site assignment: First come, first served; no reservations

Registration: Self-registration on site

Facilities: Water spigot, pump well, vault toilets

Parking: At campsites and visitor parking area

Fee: $5 per night

Elevation: 3,400 feet

Restrictions:

Pets—On leash only

Fires—In fire grates only

Alcoholic beverages—At campsites only

Vehicles—None

Other—14-day stay limit

TEA CREEK

Marlinton

Tea Creek Campground used to be an old logging camp. A lot of hard labor went on here many decades ago. Now, you can come here to escape the working world. And it is no job finding fun things to do. The nearby Williams River is a mecca for trout fishing, and hikers can trek the many trails of the Tea Creek Backcountry or the Cranberry Wilderness. The Highland Scenic Highway makes a great driving trip spring, summer, or fall. Tea Creek has had some flooding problems in the past. However, do not let this deter your coming here. Just don't come if heavy rains are expected.

Cross the low water bridge over Williams River and enter the Tea Creek Recreation Area. Just across the bridge are trailheads leading into the Tea Creek Backcountry. To your right is a spur road with several campsites strewn along Tea Creek. Most of the sites are not directly creekside, but five sites are along the rushing brook. The birch, maple, and tulip tree woods here are thick in spots, with an understory of rhododendron and small trees availing good campsite privacy. The sites here are large and spacious.

Pass the campground host, then come to the road to your left. It is a loop road circling through more dense woods. The woods are so thick that campsites are not visible to one another, whether they are on

CAMPGROUND RATINGS

Beauty:	★★★
Site privacy:	★★★★
Site spaciousness:	★★★★
Quiet:	★★★★
Security:	★★★★
Cleanliness/upkeep:	★★★★

Tea Creek is at the center of many Monongahela National Forest attractions.

ALLEGHENY HIGHLANDS

the inside or outside of the loop. I recommend this loop over the other road.

Expect to have company here on summer weekends. Get here early on Saturday mornings to make sure you get a campsite. During the week campsites are available in spring, summer, or fall. It gets a lot of local use on summer holidays. Don't bother trying to risk getting a site—you won't.

Why do locals like Tea Creek? The Williams River flows right by the campground for starters. It is a good fishery, flowing for 22 miles through the national forest, that has catch and release sections, as well as catch and keep sections, where you can vie for rainbow, brown, and brook trout. Anglers will be fishing right from the bridge over the campground.

The Tea Creek Backcountry has an extensive network of trails that extend north right from the campground. There are 40 miles of pathways. If you want to hike and fish take the Williams Creek Trail, which heads upstream for 3 miles. Or you can walk upstream along Tea Creek, so named for its reddish waters, for 3 miles, then turn right on the North Face Trail, climbing into the high country to reach the Tea Creek Mountain Trail at 6 miles. It is 1.5 more miles back down to reach the Williams Creek Trail near the campground, coming in at a little over 7 miles. Take this loop and you'll be ready for a dip in the cool waters of the Williams River.

You can also make a loop with the Bannock Shoals Run Trail, the Saddle Loop Trail, and the Turkey Point Connector Trail. This one also covers the highs and lows of the mountainous surroundings and is around 9 miles. The Bannock Shoals Run Trail starts in the rear of the campground spur road.

You may feel like enjoying the mountains from your automobile. This is the place to do it. The Highland Scenic Highway runs right by Tea Creek. There are several overlooks and picnic areas along the 45-mile road. Head south and you can get great views to the east of the lands below the Allegheny Plateau. To your right is the Cranberry Wilderness. Several trails spur off the scenic highway into the Cranberry. One trail of note (High Rocks Trail) actually goes west, instead of east, into the Cranberry Wilderness. It is a 3-mile round-trip to a fantastic lookout on a rock outcrop. This well-marked trailhead is 10 miles south of Forest Road 86 at Tea Creek on the scenic highway.

Also worth a visit is the Cranberry Mountain Visitor Center. It offers more information and informative nature displays. It is 13 miles south of the Tea Creek Area on the scenic highway. With a road this tempting to drive, you may be making a few supply runs into Marlinton just to get more views.

To get there: From Marlinton, drive north on U.S. 219 for 7 miles to Highland Scenic Highway. Turn left on Highland Scenic Highway and follow it south for 10 miles to FS 86. Turn left on FS 86 and follow it a short distance to Tea Creek Campground, which will be on your right.

KEY INFORMATION

Tea Creek Campground
P.O. Box 210
Marlinton, WV 24954-0210

Operated by: U.S. Forest Service

Information: (304) 799-4334, www.fs.fed.us/r9/mon/

Open: Mid-March through mid-December

Individual sites: 29

Each site has: Picnic table, fire rings, lantern post

Site assignment: First come, first served; no reservations

Registration: Self-registration on site

Facilities: Hand-pump water, vault toilet

Parking: At campsites only

Fee: $6 per night

Elevation: 2,950 feet

Restrictions:

Pets—On leash only

Fires—In fire rings only

Alcoholic beverages—At campsites only

Vehicles—None

Other—14-day stay limit

WATOGA STATE PARK

Seebert

There is so much going on at and around Watoga State Park, the state's largest, it is hard to describe it all. First, there is the natural scenery: Appalachian Mountains in their glory carved by tumbling streams and the Greenbrier River, a clear valley stream along which runs the famed Greenbrier River Trail. Add all the birds, mammals, and fish that call such settings home. The adjacent Calvin Price State Forest essentially doubles the size of the area.

Then there are the recreation opportunities: hiking, horseback riding, swimming, tubing, mountain biking, fishing, nature programs, and organized sports on several game courts. There are educational opportunities, too. You can check out a little park history at the Civilian Conservation Corps Museum. Or learn about trees at the Brooks Arboretum. Three camping areas complete the Watoga picture. There are two separate campgrounds and one more primitive camping area. They offer different yet quality camping experiences where any camper would be proud to pitch a tent.

Beaver Creek is the original campground. Pass the check-in station and come to a camping area on your left. Several electric sites are set beneath a grassy woodland in a flat. They are of adequate size but a little close together. Farther back are larger, more secluded sites. A small playground and bathhouse are in the loops back here.

CAMPGROUND RATINGS

Beauty:	★★★
Site privacy:	★★★
Site spaciousness:	★★★
Quiet:	★★★★
Security:	★★★★★
Cleanliness/upkeep:	★★★★★

Watoga was one of West Virginia's first state parks. It is still one of the finest.

ALLEGHENY HIGHLANDS

Straight ahead on the main road are five nice sites in a more wooded area. Pass a gate and turn left. The ten campsites on this road are the park ranger's favorite sites. Across from this road is an open field.

The Riverside Campground is adjacent to the Greenbrier River, far from Beaver Creek. There are 20 waterfront sites, among a total of 48 here, shaded with hemlock, white pine, maple, and bordered with rhododendron. There is more than ample shade, even though a few sites are very open. Two bathhouses offer plenty of showering places for campers.

The third camping area, Laurel Run, is more primitive. It doesn't have water and only has vault toilets. It is near Calvin Price State Forest, where Laurel Run and Kennison Run come together. There are only 12 sites here. You can bet your bottom dollar no RVs will be here.

Watoga has a complex reservation system that is hard to explain, much less understand. Call the park if you are interested in reserving a site here. Watoga will fill on summer holidays, but only Riverside Campground fills most summer weekends. It is easier to get a site at Beaver Creek and it is nearer most park facilities except for accessing the Greenbrier River and Greenbrier River Trail. Laurel Run is almost always available.

The Greenbrier River Trail is a 75-mile rail trail. Mountain bikers love it, as it crosses numerous bridges and a couple of tunnels, while paralleling the Greenbrier River. Hikers and other nature enthusiasts use the trail, too. Anglers will be seen on the river, casting for bass. The waterway is great for tubing on a hot summer day. Tubes can be rented near the park at Jack Horner's Corner Store in Seebert.

There are 40 miles of trails inside Watoga, including a portion of the Allegheny Trail, which runs the length of the state. Enjoy great views of the Greenbrier River on the Arrowhead Trail atop the Ann Bailey Lookout Tower. Your most informative trails will be in the Brooks Arboretum area. These trails feature interpretive displays that enhance your knowledge of the woods. Of course, you can get information first-hand at Watoga during some of the interpretive programs that are held daily Memorial Day through Labor Day. Park stables allow you to travel the trails on horseback. There are guided rides every day throughout the summer months.

Killbuck Lake offers 11 acres of boating and fishing. Rowboats and paddleboats are for rent, and bass, bluegill, and trout occupy the lake for anglers. Many folks enjoy the water at the park pool. There is a recreation hall for rainy days. You can play tennis, ping-pong, croquet, badminton, horseshoes, shuffleboard, and more using park equipment. Come to think of it, you may have to stay here a long time to do everything offered here.

To get there: From Marlinton, drive south 10 miles on U.S. 219 to Seebert Road (CR 27). Turn left on Seebert Road and follow it for 2 miles to Watoga State Park.

KEY INFORMATION

Watoga State Park
HC 82, Box 252
Marlinton, WV 24954

Operated by: West Virginia State Parks

Information: (304) 799-4087, www.watoga.com

Open: April 1 through November 30

Individual sites: 30 electric, 58 nonelectric

Each site has: Most have picnic table, fire grate, lantern post, tent pad

Site assignment: Reservations are accepted, but not required

Registration: By phone or campground check-in station

Facilities: Hot showers, water spigots, coin laundry, pay phone

Parking: At campsites only

Fee: $16 per night electric, $11 per night nonelectric, $5 per night primitive sites

Elevation: 2,100 feet

Restrictions:

Pets—On leash only

Fires—In fire grates only

Alcoholic beverages—Prohibited

Vehicles—None

Other—14-day stay limit

EASTERN
PANHANDLE

BIG BEND

Petersburg

This campground lies in a dramatic setting. It is perched on a peninsula, around which the South Branch Potomac River nearly encircles the camping area. On the outside of the river, wooded cliffs rise tall to form a natural cathedral. Old-timers called this the Smoke Hole, because the mist rising from the deep gorge reminded them of smoke emerging from a cavity in the ground. The South Branch Potomac River attracts anglers vying for trout and smallmouth bass. Around the campground you'll see folks fiddling with rods, hanging up waders, and telling fishing tales. But even if you don't like to fish, this is a great destination. The setting can hardly be beat, and trails leave the campground and nearby vicinity. Also, the campground itself is attractive and heavy on campsite privacy.

The drive here is "gorge-ous" and Big Bend only gets better. Enter the campground and look above at the mountain wall around you. Turn left, pass the campground host, and come to the River Loop. An old cemetery is off to your right, encircled by a wood fence. The River Loop is set in a plain along the river. It was once a field and is growing up in white pine, sycamore, autumn olive, and a hodgepodge of other forest trees. Campsites are very dispersed. The forest service is keeping the area naturalized; many small trees and bushes provide dense cover and campsite privacy. The riverside campsites don't offer direct views

CAMPGROUND RATINGS

Beauty:	★★★★★
Site privacy:	★★★★★
Site spaciousness:	★★★
Quiet:	★★★★
Security:	★★★★
Cleanliness/upkeep:	★★★★

Camp down in the canyon of the Smoke Hole.

EASTERN PANHANDLE

of the river. However, the gorge is visible all around you.

The Upper Loop climbs the main road onto a hill. There are actually two loops. Enter the first loop, which has 17 campsites. White pines and autumn olive grow in great abundance here, too. Locust trees also indicate this was a former field. But what you'll notice is that the density of the forest allows views of your campsite only.

The sites up here do not have tent pads, but just like the sites below, there are water spigots everywhere and a nice bathhouse for your convenience. The forest is thick, but the grass around the campsites is mowed regularly. The strange mix of trees here range from balsam to cedar to red bud. Some of the sites are set far back from the road.

The second upper loop is the highest and farthest from the river. It is much like the first upper loop. The dense, mixed forest continues. Campsite #39 is the very apex of the campground; land drops off all around it. From this point it is downhill for the remainder of the loop.

Fishing is a big draw here. The South Branch Potomac River is a good fishery, but even if you get skunked, the music of the river and the sight of the Smoke Hole are keepers. There are other ways to enjoy the river. Canoeing is a great way to get on the water and be right in the middle of the Smoke Hole Canyon. Eagles Nest Outfitter is just outside Petersburg and has been in business for over 20 years. The outfitter specializes in river trips on the South Branch Potomac River ranging from one hour to several days. Some river runs are dependent upon water levels. Call them at (304) 257-2393 or visit the Web at wvweb.com/www/eaglesnest for more information.

Closer to your campsite is the Big Bend Loop Trail. It makes a 1-mile circle around the river and over the hill behind the campground. Anglers and bird watchers enjoy the canyon views. The chimney you pass is the remnant of an old post office. Another nearby hike is South Branch Trail. The 3.5-mile loop starts at the Smoke Hole Picnic Area, which you passed on the way in. Follow the river downstream, then cut back up the ridge, passing fields and an old homestead, then drop back down to the picnic area. Good views of the Smoke Hole Canyon can be found here, and this is what the Big Bend experience is all about.

To get there: From Petersburg, drive south on U.S. 220 for 12 miles to CR 2, which is just after a bridge crossing over South Branch Potomac River. Turn right on CR 2 and follow it 9 miles until it dead-ends at Big Bend Campground.

KEY INFORMATION

Big Bend Campground
HC 59, Box 240
Petersburg, WV 26847

Operated by: U.S. Forest Service

Information: (304) 257-4488, reservations (877) 444-6777, www.fs.fed.us/r9/mon/

Open: April 15 through October 31

Individual sites: 46

Each site has: Picnic table, fire grate, lantern post; River Loop also has tent pad

Site assignment: First come, first served unless reserved

Registration: By phone or with campground host

Facilities: Hot showers, flush toilets, water spigots

Parking: At campsites only

Fee: $13 per night River Loop, $11 per night Upper Loop

Elevation—1,200 feet

Restrictions:

  *Pets—*On leash only

  Fires— In fire rings only

  *Alcoholic beverages—*At campsites only

  *Vehicles—*None

  *Other—*14-day stay limit

BLACKWATER FALLS STATE PARK

Davis

This could be called high livin' in the high country. Take the panoramic Potomac Highlands, with its cold, clear rivers, open fields offering mountain vistas, dense spruce-fir woodlands, and then carve a state park out of some of the best scenery in the state. The campground itself is nothing to shout about from the mountaintops, but the mountaintop landscape will leave you breathless. It has the park's namesake waterfall, awesome views into the Blackwater River Canyon, good hiking and biking, and other amenities that are more down-to-earth.

Let's start with the campground. It is high and cool. Bring an extra sweater and a warm sleeping bag, even in the summer. Most nights will bring you closer to the campfire, especially in spring and fall.

The campground is divided into two loops. The right-hand loop has electricity. This means bigger rigs, but on my visit there weren't many at all. Twenty of these 30 sites can be reserved. This loop is set on a plateau forest of northern hardwoods in an area that is open and grassy. The first few sites are well wooded, but the latter half of the loop is very open, which can mean lots of sun and/or wind exposure. In the center of this loop is the heated bathhouse. Water spigots are set throughout the campground. The sites are not especially spacious or level, but there are a few desirable sites.

CAMPGROUND RATINGS

Beauty:	★★★
Site privacy:	★★★
Site spaciousness:	★★★
Quiet:	★★★★
Security:	★★★★★
Cleanliness/upkeep:	★★★★★

This is the highest state park campground in the book. And the surrounding scenery is some of the best, too.

EASTERN PANHANDLE

The left-hand loop has more vertical variation, yet it surprisingly has more good sites. The beginning of the loop slopes down, but then rises back up. Most campsites have enough woods around them for adequate shade and privacy. But I wouldn't want to spend the night fighting gravity on some of these sloping sites. Be picky and you can get a good site. The last half of the loop is much more level, as is evidenced by the many disabled-accessible sites near the unheated bathhouse. All the

sites on this loop, the loop most tent campers prefer, are first come, first served. Blackwater Falls fills on major summer holidays and an average of every other weekend during the summer, depending on the weather.

Your first stop should be the park's namesake. There are two ways to view it. Take the Gentle Trail a short distance or take the trail from the Trading Post, a souvenir shop. Either way, the 65-foot falls will make you want more canyon scenery. You can see the Falls of Ekakala and a shot of the Blackwater River Canyon from Ekakala Trail. The Ekakala Trail starts near the park lodge, where you can dine in style after your evening stroll. Make the short walk to Pendleton Point for a view of the lower canyon. The Balanced Rock Trail goes to an odd rock formation where one rock looks like it is a single rock balancing on top of another rock. Get a trail map from the campground registration station.

Many campers like to bike around the park and environs. Some backcountry trails allow bikes, but the park roads are really fun, and easier, too. If you want some challenging biking, try the Canaan Loop Road, which leaves the park and enters the Monongahela National Forest. The gravel road itself is fun to ride, and other trails spur off it. The road is open to vehicles, but I wouldn't bother unless I had a four-wheel-drive vehicle on the section closest to Blackwater Falls. The Blackwater River offers both catch-and-keep and special catch-and-release fishing. The Department of Natural Resources stocks the canyon by helicopter. That is a sight to see.

Man-made diversions include swimming Pendleton Lake, where there is a beach. The beach is open Memorial Day through Labor Day. You can fish it, too, for bass and bluegill. There are tennis courts, volleyball courts, and basketball courts in the vicinity. Also, near this area is the park's Nature Center. During summer months, the park offers daily nature and recreation programs led by a naturalist. Take advantage of this. You can learn a lot from a naturalist. Knowledge will enhance your appreciation for the Potomac Highlands and Blackwater Falls State Park.

To get there: From Harmon, drive north on WV 32 for 20 miles to the town of Davis. Once in Davis, turn left at the sign for Blackwater Falls and soon enter the park.

KEY INFORMATION

Blackwater Falls State Park
P.O. Box 490
Davis, WV 26260

Operated by: West Virginia State Parks

Information: (304) 259-5216, www.blackwaterfalls.com

Open: May 1 through October 31

Individual sites: 45 electric, 25 nonelectric

Each site has: Picnic table, fire ring

Site assignment: First come, first served unless reserved

Registration: By phone or at campground registration station

Facilities: Hot showers, flush toilets, coin laundry, pay phone

Parking: At campsites only

Fee: $11 per night nonelectric, $16 per night electric

Elevation: 3,100 feet

Restrictions:

Pets—On leash only

Fires—In fire rings only

Alcoholic beverages—At campsites only

Vehicles—None

Other—14-day stay limit; one tent per site

BRANDYWINE LAKE

Brandywine

The town of Brandywine, 3 miles from the campground, benefits from this campground and recreation area. Sure, it has a great location for camping, hiking, and fishing, but also the tall dam that forms Brandywine Lake has filled to the brim twice since 1964, when it was built. That may not seem impressive until you see how high the dam is in comparison to the size of Brandywine Lake. If it wasn't for that dam, the town of Brandywine might not be here. But don't let potential flooding scare you away from here. Any slice of flat ground in West Virginia, and there aren't many in the Mountain State, is capable of flooding.

Enter the attractive Hawes Run valley. The big dam and pretty lake will be on your right. The white sand beach contrasts the green grass of the picnic area. Pass by the new bathhouse for the picnic area and the campground and enter the camping area proper, set alongside Hawes Run. The lines of development are crisp and clean with the makeover, and mesh well with the woodland. The paved loop road and paved pull-ins make the campground less dusty. Landscaping timbers delineate the large, level graveled sites, which act as an oversized tent pad for your entire camping area. Overhead, a white pine–dominated forest lends plenty of shade. Numerous immature trees act as campsite barriers. The main road divides, then comes together, and seven campsites are spread far apart here.

CAMPGROUND RATINGS

Beauty:	★★★★
Site privacy:	★★★★
Site spaciousness:	★★★★★
Quiet:	★★★★
Security:	★★★★
Cleanliness/upkeep:	★★★★

Brandywine Lake is a fully developed national forest facility that has received a makeover. Now it's even better.

EASTERN PANHANDLE

The ultra-large sites are spaced well apart.

There is one more bathhouse and two more vault toilets up here. Plenty of water spigots are dispersed about. More campsites are laid out along Hawes Run. The hollow widens with the addition of a side branch. The camping area also widens and makes a final loop. These are the best sites back here. At the head of this loop is a grassy field that houses the group camp and overflow campsites.

No reservations are accepted here. Most national forest campgrounds this nice have gone to a reservation system. However, barring major holidays, you should get a campsite if you arrive on a Friday before 6 p.m. Getting a site is no problem during the week. After October 1, services (and the prices) are reduced to only pump well water and vault toilets. A trailer dump station may attract a few big rigs, but don't let that bother you. No electricity or sewage hookups or reservations keep their numbers way down.

The dam-to-lake size ratio will impress you, but so will Brandywine Lake itself. It is a ten-acre clear impoundment backed against Cowger Mountain. Attractive picnic areas are near the lake. On summer days adults lounge by the beach, watching the kids play. Others fish for trout around the lake. No gas motors are allowed on the water.

Brandywine has an excellent hiking loop trail that is the right distance for nearly all tent campers. The 3.6-mile Sawmill Trail leaves the upper camping loop and makes a loop of its own. Parallel Hawes Run, crossing it four times and passing the site of a sawmill at mile 1.1. Cross Hawes Run one more time before winding across a couple of low ridges and circling some clearings.

These clearings are wildlife food plots. When clearings are made, this creates "edges," places where two plant habitats meet. These edges are richer in food sources for wildlife than either of the two habitats individually. Make this 3.6-mile loop in the morning, and you may see wildlife, such as turkeys or deer, near one of these edges.

Most people come here for the mountain-rimmed lake and its offerings. There might not be many people around here at all, including nearby residents, if it wasn't for the lake. The folks in Brandywine are glad it's here; you will be, too.

To get there: From the town of Brandywine, turn east on U.S. 33 and follow it for 3 miles to Brandywine Recreation Area, which will be on your right.

KEY INFORMATION

Brandywine Lake
112 North River Road
Bridgewater, VA 22812

Operated by: U.S. Forest Service

Information: (540) 828-2591, www.fs.fed.us/gwjnf

Open: Full services: May 15 through September 30; Reduced services: October 1 through November 30

Individual sites: 34

Each site has: Picnic table, fire grate, tent pad, lantern post

Site assignment: First come, first served; no reservations

Registration: Self-registration on site

Facilities: Hot showers, flush toilets, vault toilets, water spigots

Parking: At campsites only

Fee: $10 per night May 15 through September 30; $5 per night October 1 through November 30

Elevation: 2,000 feet

Restrictions:

Pets—On leash only

Fires—In fire grates only

Alcoholic beverages—At campsites only

Vehicles—None

Other—14-day stay limit

CAMP RUN

Brandywine

Do you remember the television show *Seinfeld?* Its premise was "a show about nothing." Apparently they did something, because the show was on a long time. That could be the premise for Camp Run Campground. Camping here is about doing nothing. The campground is extremely primitive and rough—the gravel of the campground road is minimal, the campsites aren't numbered, there's no registration, no bulletin board telling you of things to do, and there's no fee.

On the surface it does seem there is nothing to do here. Oh, you could fish Camp Run and Little Camp Run. Or you could fish Camp Run Lake below the campground. But why bother? Just come here and do nothing but perfect the lost art of true outdoor camping. True outdoor camping—where you overnight in a tent and enjoy the natural world around you by day—is possible even when the weather doesn't exactly cooperate. When it's cold, you perfect your fire-building techniques or grill out. When it's rainy, you get a tarp set up just right and play cards or read a book, every once in while looking out at the downpour and getting a laugh out of being satisfactorily dry. Or when the weather is ideal, you get out your tree identification book and finally set about learning what these big tall plants are all around you that make you feel so relaxed. Or maybe it is finally getting to spend

CAMPGROUND RATINGS

Beauty:	★★★★
Site privacy:	★★★★
Site spaciousness:	★★★
Quiet:	★★★★
Security:	★★★
Cleanliness/upkeep:	★★★

Camp Run is the least developed and most primitive campsite in this entire guidebook.

EASTERN PANHANDLE

some uninterrupted time in a peaceful setting with those about whom you care most.

Camp Run has been a good place to pitch a tent for a long time, judging by its name. The camping area is set just below the confluence of Camp Run and Little Camp Run. A high mountainside looms to your right, and Camp Run flows along to your left. A level, pretty hollow runs up to the mountainside, and this is where the campsites lie. The ten campsites, each with picnic table, concrete fire grate with a

grill attached, lantern post, and tent pad, are far back from the road. Two sites on the small turnaround at the head of the campground are especially attractive. The oak-hickory-pine forest is tall overhead.

A vault toilet for each gender are the only amenities. The pump well has been capped. But this place is clean. A national forest program enlists senior citizens to come out once a week, volunteering their time, to make sure this campground is clean. Do your part and make their job easier. There are trash cans, but I suggest using the "pack it in, pack it out" philosophy here.

People live in the nearby area, but it is a very isolated campground. Make sure and bring in your supplies or you'll be running the roads back to Franklin. By the way, the valleys and mountains of this part of West Virginia are among the state's prettiest.

Fishing is the only thing you can do directly from the campground. But if you want to go hiking, head to Lost River State Park. Take Route 3 north to County Road 12. Turn right on CR 12 and follow this pretty road with lots of views over South Branch Mountain to the state park. They have over 18 miles of trails there. You can also see the old Lee Cabin and eat at the park restaurant.

They don't have a park-run campground. So maybe you could stay at Camp Run and hike at Lost River State Park. Maybe not. When I stayed at Camp Run, I did nothing, not a thing.

> To get there: From Brandywine, head north on U.S. 33. Follow it 3.3 miles to Route 3 in Oak Flat. Turn right on Route 3 and follow it 10 miles to Route 3/1 (Camp Run Road). Follow the gravel road 1.5 miles, passing Camp Run Lake to Camp Run Campground, which will be on your right.

KEY INFORMATION

Camp Run Campground
112 North River Road
Bridgewater, VA 22812

Operated by: U.S. Forest Service

Information: (540) 828-2591, www.fs.fed.us/gwjnf

Open: Year-round

Individual sites: 10

Each site has: Picnic table, fire grate, tent pad, lantern post

Site assignment: First come, first served; no reservations

Registration: No registration

Facilities: Vault toilets (bring water)

Parking: At campsites only

Fee: None

Elevation: 1,800 feet

Restrictions:

Pets—On leash only

Fires—In fire grates only

Alcoholic beverages—At campsites only

Vehicles—None

Other—14-day stay limit

HAWK

Wardensville

Hawk lies in a remote corner of West Virginia in a remote corner of the George Washington National Forest. However, I found my way here. And when I pulled up to Hawk my first thought was, "I can't believe this campground is free!" Then I made a loop, found a site, and began to enjoy an ideal spring day. Dogwoods, a major understory tree in this campground, were blooming everywhere. A literal profusion of creamy blossoms dotted the woodland. Overhead, the oak, maple, and hickory trees were just budding. This place is loaded with oaks— northern white oak, scarlet oak, and black oak. I actually got out my tree book and began to identify just how many oaks there were. The answer? A lot.

This is one of the nicest free national forest campgrounds I've seen anywhere. Situated in the most northwestern slice of the George Washington National Forest, it seems to have been forgotten. But it hasn't been left to fall into disrepair. Quite the contrary, the campsites were just as good as a pay campground; the pump well and vault toilets were fine; the picnic area and group campground were also in good condition.

Great North Mountain, the dividing line between West Virginia and Virginia here, rises just a few miles east. Hawk is set on a flat of the mountain slope. A little stream runs nearby, but this is an upland forest with a western exposure, hence all the

CAMPGROUND RATINGS

Beauty: ★★★★
Site privacy: ★★★★
Site spaciousness: ★★★★★
Quiet: ★★★★★
Security: ★★★
Cleanliness/upkeep: ★★★★

It's hard to believe this campground is free.

EASTERN PANHANDLE

oaks. Enter the campground loop and pass the first of two vault toilets for each gender. Notice how the campsites are so large and well dispersed. Large stones delineate the parking areas. The tent pads are graveled for good drainage.

The first few sites have the least tree cover. Yet there is still adequate shade, except at high noon. The slope increases past campsite #6. However, a little stone work levels the parking and camping areas. The sites toward the end of the loop look down into the woods and are heavily shaded. A few sites are on the inside of the loop, but there is not a bad site here.

Campsite use is little to nil during the week. A site can be found nearly every weekend, especially during the cooler times of the year. Since the forest service garners no revenue from this campground, there is no garbage service. It is a "pack it in, pack it out" campground. Do your part to keep it as nice as when I spent my early May day.

I suggest coming here during the spring or fall. Summertime might be too hot at this 1,400 foot elevation, especially with no water to speak of nearby. Besides, the shoulder seasons are a good time to hike. And the Tuscarora Trail passes right by the campground. This is a long-distance trail that goes from Virginia to Pennsylvania via West Virginia. It was designed as an alternative long-distance trail to the Appalachian Trail.

Walk back to the campground entrance. Across the road is a blue-blazed trail. To your right, running by the picnic area, is also a blue-blazed trail. This is the Tuscarora. A right turn will take you downhill and downstream for a 1.5-mile walk to Hawk Run. There are some small falls along the stream. You can keep from backtracking by cutting west and returning up one of the gated roads back toward Hawk.

The most popular hike on the Tuscarora goes left, uphill, winding back and forth up the slope of Great North Mountain, reaching the crest at 1.8 mile. Keep on, crossing a couple of roads, then coming to a rock outcrop and view at 3.8 miles. If you continue, there is a trail shelter at 4.3 miles. A side trail descends to a spring here, if you need water. This hike may or may not stimulate you to try such a walk as the length of the state. There is also another closer, shorter walk. The Margaret Gollady Wild Flower Trail leaves the campground near campsite #6. It was so new when I walked it that I couldn't follow it. I hope it is better marked by now.

Even as out-of-the-way as the campground feels, the town of Wardensville and its stores are just a few miles away. Yet Wardensville seems more like a world away from the oaks and dogwoods at Hawk.

To get there: From Wardensville, drive east on WV 55 for 4 miles. Turn left on FS 502 and follow it for 3 miles to FS 347, your first left, for .8 mile to Hawk Recreation Area, which will be on your right.

KEY INFORMATION

Hawk Recreation Area
109 Molineau Road
Edinburgh, VA 22834
Operated by: U.S. Forest Service

Information: (540) 984-4101

Open: Year-round

Individual sites: 10

Each site has: Picnic table, fire ring, lantern post, tent pad

Site assignment: First come, first served; no reservations

Registration: Self-registration on site

Facilities: Pump well, vault toilets

Parking: At campsites only

Fee: None

Elevation: 1,400 feet

Restrictions:

Pets—On leash only

Fires—In fire ring only

Alcoholic beverages—At campsites only

Vehicles—None

Other—21-day stay limit

RED CREEK

Petersburg

This is one of the highest campgrounds in the state—perched at nearly 4,000 feet, atop the same high plateau that houses the Dolly Sods. The flora and climate are more like Canada than West Virginia. On my trip here in early May, most of the trees had not yet begun to leaf out. It is a whole different world from the "lowlands" below. The air cools significantly as you drive up the plateau. Snow is a possibility here eight months of the year. Freezing temperatures can occur anytime of the year. This is not to scare you off. Rather, Red Creek can be a refreshing break during the long, hot summer. But bring warm clothes all the same.

Maybe you can keep warm by hiking, because the Dolly Sods is laced with trails. These trails pass through spruce thickets, northern hardwood forests, and many open areas known as plains. The forest here was once logged, and fires followed. In many areas the topsoil was burned to the rock below. These areas have remained treeless and add to the beauty and scenery. Vistas seem to be everywhere.

I like this campground. It is small and rustic. Campsites are well dispersed, and you can actually go hiking right from your tent. Two small creeks converge in the campground. The campground is in a northern hardwood forest. Cherry, yellow birch, red maple, serviceberry, beech, a few spruce, and aspens—a rarity this far south—adorn the area. The forest is fairly

CAMPGROUND RATINGS

Beauty:	★★★★
Site privacy:	★★★
Site spaciousness:	★★★
Quiet:	★★★★★
Security:	★★★
Cleanliness/upkeep:	★★★★

Red Creek is highland headquarters for exploring the Dolly Sods Wilderness and Scenic Area.

EASTERN PANHANDLE

young, and many of trees have a stunted look. Some campsites can be sunny at high noon.

Enter the loop and the first campsite is wide open. But then you come to a parking area for two walk-in tent sites. Take a short path to these sites that are set apart from the rest of the campground. These are ideal for tenters who want the most in privacy. Beyond this, the sites are well dispersed. Some are set far back from the road.

A small bridge connects campers in the back of the loop to the modern vault toilets in the center of the loop. The pump well is also here, toward the front of the loop. This small campground will fill on major holidays, but is weather dependent. Nice weekends can bring people out. Most campers here are active folks who want to explore the wealth of unusual West Virginia beauty around them.

The Dolly Sods Wilderness is 10,000 acres of exceptional country. The Dolly Sods Scenic Area adjoins the wilderness and is much the same as the wilderness. A great hike for campers is the Blackbird Knob Trail. It starts just outside the campground. Take the path and head through some thick woods before soon opening up to great views of the mountains and plains around you. Cross Alder Branch and the Red Creek before emerging onto another flat field. Continue beyond this, passing the Red Creek Trail, which splits off to the left. Keep forward and skirt the edge of Blackbird Knob. Climb the open hill to your right amid a boulder field. There are stupendous views of the Red Creek gorge and the Allegheny Mountains stretching off to the southwest.

Just south of the campground is the Northland Loop Trail. It is a 0.4-mile, interpretive trail that gives you an idea of the region's ecology. Back a ways on Forest Road 75 are several trails that enter Dolly Sods. The Rohrbough

Plains Trail offers very good overlooks about 2 miles from the road. You can make a loop using the Rohrbough Plains Trail, the Wildlife Trail, and FS 75. The Red Creek Trail is the backbone of the trail system in the Dolly Sods. You can catch this trail from Blackbird Knob, or drive south from the campground to Forest Road 19 toward Laneville and start your hike from the bottom up.

Actually, with this much open terrain here, off-trail hiking is an option. But if you want to experience a different side of West Virginia, passing by Dolly Sods and Red Creek Campground is not an option.

To get there: From Petersburg, drive West on WV 28 for 8.5 miles to Jordan Run Road (CR 28/7). Turn right on Jordan Run Road and follow it for 1 mile to FS 19, which will be on your left. Turn left on FS 19 and follow it for 6 miles to FS 75. Turn right on FS 75 and follow it for 5 miles to Red Run, which will be on your left.

KEY INFORMATION

Red Creek Campround
HC 59, Box 240
Petersburg, WV 26847

Operated by: U.S. Forest Service

Information: (304) 257-4488, www.fs.fed.us/r9/mon/

Open: Mid-April through November 30

Individual sites: 12

Each site has: Picnic table, fire ring, lantern post

Site assignment: First come, first served; no reservations

Registration: Self-registration on site

Facilities: Pump well, vault toilets

Parking: At campsites and walk-in tent camper parking area only

Fee: $10 per night

Elevation: 3,900 feet

Restrictions:

Pets—On leash only

Fires—In fire rings only

Alcoholic beverages—At campsites only

Vehicles—None

Other—14-day stay limit

SENECA SHADOWS

Seneca Rocks

This is one of the forest service's newer campgrounds, and the layout and facilities show it. And they sure picked the right place to put it—perched on a hill with a million-dollar view of Seneca Rocks. This view is reserved for the walk-in tent sites only. The rest of the campground has to settle for a high-quality camping area adjacent to many forest activities and other nearby attractions. You're a winner no matter where you stay at Seneca Shadows.

Drive the paved road past the seldom-used registration station and come to Loop A. Turn right and descend in an oak-hickory forest. Campsites are spread on either side of the road, which ends in a small turnaround. Even though the terrain is sloped, the campsites are not. The paved pull-ins are level, and so are the gravel-and-sand tent pads. Some sites have wooden steps on them to access the tent pad or picnic table. Site spaciousness is no problem, and an understory of smaller trees and brush keeps the sites private. A fully-equipped bathhouse with a water spigot completes the picture.

Loop B is much like Loop A, only it is farther down the main road. The campsites here are very dispersed, and the vertical variation between sites adds to the campsite privacy. Pass the road to the amphitheater and come to Loop C. This camping area splits off into two roads. The terrain is

CAMPGROUND RATINGS

Beauty:	★★★★★
Site privacy:	★★★
Site spaciousness:	★★★★
Quiet:	★★★★
Security:	★★★★★
Cleanliness/upkeep:	★★★★★

The walk-in tent sites here have a majestic view of Seneca Rocks.

EASTERN PANHANDLE

more level and the 13 camp-sites are equipped with electricity. There is a toilet and a bathhouse here.

Pass the group camp and come to the tent camper's parking area. Walk a short path to the far side of a row of trees and come to the tent campers' area. It is in a level, grassy field. Off to your right, in plain view for every tent camper, are Seneca Rocks. Next to the row of trees is a row of tent sites. The center of the field is left naturalized in growing grass. Across this grass are more tent sites. Up on a hill to your left are a few sites that have the grandest view of them all. Down the hill are even more tent sites. Each of these 40 sites are well marked and delineated. A few trees dot the area, but little shade is available. Planners just couldn't stand to wreck the view. And I understand.

There are vault toilets by the parking area. Showers are a short walk away in the bathhouse for Loop C. A covered pavilion in the tent camper's area is perfect for cooking on rainy days.

Looking at those rocks just drives folks to surmount them. There is a steep, 1.3-mile foot trail to Seneca Rocks, which rise 900 feet above the valley floor. The trail starts near the expanded visitor center, where there are interpretive displays and forest information. There are also interpretive programs at the campground on summer weekends.

Rock climbers often stay at the campground. Then they will attack Seneca Rocks, with ropes and harnesses and helmets, heading upward. If you would like to rock climb, there is a rock climbing school a mile away in the town of

Seneca Rocks. From April to October, learn to climb from Seneca Rocks Climbing School, or if you have some experience, go on a guided climb. Their phone number is (800) 548-0108.

If you don't want to climb, then head underground. Go on a guided tour of Seneca Caverns. See all the weird rock formations and Mirror Lake. This cavern is south of the campground on U.S. 33. The whole area is pretty, and Seneca Rocks are especially scenic. If the views here don't inspire you, it's time to put the tent up for sale.

To get there: From the town of Seneca Rocks, drive south on U.S. 33 for 1.5 miles. The campground will be on your right.

---

(304) 567 3082

Seneca Shadows
HC 59, Box 240
Petersburg, WV 26847

Operated by: U.S. Forest Service

Information: (304) 257-4488, reservations (877) 444-6777, www.fs.fed.us/r9/mon/

Open: April 15 through October 31

Individual sites: 13 electric, 65 nonelectric

Each site has: Picnic table, fire ring, tent pad, lantern post

Site assignment: First come, first served unless reserved

Registration: By phone or with campground host

Facilities: Hot showers, flush and vault toilets, water spigots

Parking: At campsites or tenter's parking area

Fee: $6 per night walk-in tent area, $11 per night standard campsite, $2 electricity

Elevation: 1,600 feet

Restrictions:

Pets—On leash only

Fires—In fire rings only

Alcoholic beverages—At camp-sites only

Vehicles—None

Other—14-day stay limit

SLEEPY CREEK

Martinsburg

T his area of West Virginia is dominated by long north-south running ridges with valleys between them. You will learn this lesson well, coming to Sleepy Creek from Martinsburg. Sleepy Creek Lake itself is situated in a narrow valley between Third Hill Mountain and Sleepy Creek Mountain. Sleepy Creek and Third Hill Mountains are connected by a ridge named Lock-of-the-Mountain.

This was originally a state forest. Before that it had been logged out and hunted out. Now, there is a lake rimmed in forested mountains filled with trails in the 23,000-acre area. The four campgrounds do not match the scenery, but they will do, especially for the price—$5. Hiking and fishing are the main activities for most tent campers. Check with the wildlife manager for the best and safest times to enter the woods here.

One of the major differences between a state forest and a wildlife management area is the primary reason they are managed. Most West Virginia state forests are managed for timber, then recreation. Most WMAs are managed for wildlife and hunting, then recreation. State parks are managed for preservation and recreation, not necessarily in that order. What this means for us tent campers is that WMAs can be very scenic and rewarding places to camp and have fun. We just must be a little more careful about when we come and

CAMPGROUND RATINGS

Beauty:	★★
Site privacy:	★★★
Site spaciousness:	★★★
Quiet:	★★★★★
Security:	★★★
Cleanliness/upkeep:	★★★

This is the best in tent camping in West Virginia's far east.

EASTERN PANHANDLE

understand that the camping is liable to be on the more primitive end of the spectrum.

There are many trails at Sleepy Creek. The most prominent is the Tuscarora Trail. This long-distance trail runs the length of the state. A 20-mile section of this blue-blazed pathway runs the length of the area. Sleepy Creek Lake, a long narrow impoundment with many snags in it, is the centerpiece of the whole area. Angling is a peaceful experience here, as no motors are allowed in the lake.

Drive down from Third Hill Mountain and come to the lake. The campground farthest to the right is the 22-site Lower Campground. This camp is set in a very young and open forest on a knoll. The views here are pretty good. The sun could dominate the camping experience here, which could be desirable on a cool winter day.

The next campground is Piney Point. This area is near the lake. The first three campsites are in a field next to some woods. Next are several campsites right together, too close together, overlooking the lake. There is one good solo site next to the lake.

The Myers Place Campground is near an old homesite. Drop off onto a spit of land jutting into the lake. Some of the campsites are up on the hill and other campsites are beneath young woods by the lake.

The 13-site Upper Campground has sunny and shady sites. There are several lakeside campsites under the piney woods. These are the best campsites here. The whole place has a primitive, rough look. With 75 sites, you can get a campsite any day of the year. Many sites looked little used. Bring all your supplies in, including water, though the Myers Spring is a potential source of liquid refreshment.

The Tuscarora Trail leaves on the gated road south from the Upper Campground. Here you cross Roaring Run and can continue on the Roaring Run Trail to head uphill on the Tuscarora Trail. If you take the Tuscarora Trail the other way, pass the lake and campgrounds and connect to other area trails that are just now being named and signed. Other trails designated for mountain bikers and equestrians are blazed in red.

The jewel of this place is the lake. There are 205 acres of water from which mountains rise above and fish swim below. Bring your canoe and paddle right from your campsite, if you get a lakeside spot. I was overwhelmed by the quiet, early morning here. It was just the birds. No wind or anything. Anglers can vie for northern pike, largemouth bass, bluegill, and crappie. If you are bait fishing with a bobber it will be hard to keep your eyes on the cork with the scenery around you.

To get there: From Exit 15 on I-81 in Martinsburg, take CR 13 west over North Mountain. The main paved road over the mountain changes to CR 15, then CR 18, but stay with the main road. Continue through the 4-way stop at Shanghai, and climb Third Hill Mountain. After a total of 12 miles from Martinsburg, come to the sign for Sleepy Creek Lake at the top of the mountain. Turn right at Park Road (#826) and follow it 5 miles to the lake.

KEY INFORMATION

Sleepy Creek
1910 Sleepy Creek Road
Hedgesville, WV 25427

Operated by: West Virginia Division of Natural Resources

Information: (304) 754-3855, www.dnr.state.wv.us

Open: Year-round

Individual sites: 75

Each site has: Fire ring, lantern post

Site assignment: First come, first served; no reservations

Registration: Self-registration on site

Facilities: Vault toilets, hand-pump well

Parking: At campsites only

Fee: $5 per night

Elevation: 1,100 feet

Restrictions:

Pets—On leash only

Fires—In fire rings only

Alcoholic beverages—Prohibited

Vehicles—17-foot trailer limit

Other—14-day stay limit

TROUT POND

Wardensville

West Virginia's only natural lake, Trout Pond, is a water-filled sinkhole amid some of the state's prettiest countryside. This forest service recreation area was tastefully integrated into the setting. There are fun things to do here. The facilities are clean and well maintained, especially the campground. Once here, you will agree this corner of the Mountain State is worth at least one weekend of your life.

Trout Pond Campground is situated on a mountain flat in a pretty dry forest of oak, hickory, dogwood, and a few pine trees. Many small trees and brush give the campground a feel of being gently set into the woods as opposed to bulldozing a campground area, laying out campsites, then planting a few trees to make the camping area look like it is in a forest. Some campgrounds are built this way. Not this one.

Drive into the loop. The first ten sites are on both sides of the road and have electricity. Campsites are very well delineated and are bordered with landscaping timbers to keep the natural and camping areas separate. Pass the first of three modern bathhouses with full facilities.

The campground is new, but it has old-fashioned fire rings of stone that have been concreted together for that rustic look. But they have the addition of a small circular grate attached on the edge to a post, making the grate vertically adjustable for cooking. The pull-ins are paved, as are the

CAMPGROUND RATINGS

Beauty:	★★★★
Site privacy:	★★★
Site spaciousness:	★★★★
Quiet:	★★★★
Security:	★★★★★
Cleanliness/upkeep:	★★★★

Trout Pond is West Virginia's only natural lake. Some man made amenities add to the setting.

EASTERN PANHANDLE

campground roads. This cuts down on the dust. The road splits and the electric sites end, keeping the RVs in their own part of the campground. A small stream bisects the campground.

The outer road has 21 of the best tent sites. They are most into the woods and farthest from the action. The inner road has ten nice campsites, but they have campers on both sides of them. However, all the sites in the campground have adequate site privacy and spaciousness.

Both electric and nonelectric sites can be reserved. Only ten sites are available on a first come, first served basis. Make reservations if you are coming here on a summer weekend or holiday and ask for a site numbered 15–22. These are my favorites. Even though this is a new campground by national forest standards, many of the campers told me they are repeat visitors, which is always a good sign.

It's hard to add to the beauty of an area such as this, but I have to hand it to the forest service. Rockcliff Lake is pretty. This 17-acre man-made body of water attracts swimmers and anglers alike. The white sandy beach looked like a good swimming launch, but the weather was a little too cool for me that day. Folks were fishing for trout. No gas motors are allowed on the lake, making for a peaceful setting. Nearby Trout Pond also has trout. Imagine that, but there is a limit of four fish per day.

A trail leads from the campground to Trout Pond and continues to Rockcliff Lake. The Rockcliff Lake Trail makes a 1-mile loop around the impoundment, passing rock outcrops and going over the dam. For a short geology lesson, take the Trout Pond Trail. It leaves right from the campground and goes two ways. Go left from the campground to see some of the sinkholes and depressions that are common in the area. You can make about a 2.5-mile loop by turning left on the Chimney Rock Trail and returning to the campground via Rockcliff Lake.

More ambitious hikers can make a 7-mile loop. Go right on Trout Pond Trail and turn left at Road 59, then left again on the Long Mountain Trail, then left again to intersect the far side of the Trout Pond Trail. Get a Trout Pond Recreation Area map from the forest service or the campground hosts, who look out for things during spring and summer.

Before you arrive, get supplies. There are none available nearby. Besides, once here, why leave until you have had your fill of the campground by West Virginia's only natural lake?

To get there: From Wardensville, drive south on WV 259 for 18 miles to the hamlet of Lost River. Turn left on Mill Gap/Thorn Bottom Road, CR 16, and follow it for 5 miles to FS 500. Turn right on FS 500 and follow it 1.7 miles to the gate of Trout Pond Recreation Area.

KEY INFORMATION

Trout Pond Recreation Area
109 Molineau Road
Edinburgh, VA 22834

Operated by: U.S. Forest Service

Information: (540) 984-4101, reservations (877) 444-6777, www.fs.fed.us/gwjnf

Open: Late April through late November

Individual sites: 16 electric, 34 nonelectric

Each site has: Picnic table, fire ring, lantern post, tent pad

Site assignment: First come, first served unless reserved

Registration: By phone or at entrance booth

Facilities: Warm showers, flush toilets, water spigots

Parking: At campsites only

Fee: $17 per night nonelectric, $20 per night electric

Elevation: 2,100 feet

Restrictions:

Pets—On leash only

Fires—In fire rings only

Alcoholic beverages—At campsites only

Vehicles—None

Other—14-day stay limit

WOLF GAP

Wardensville

We all know that West Virginia was once part of old Virginia. I am glad that the state line is where it is, making Wolf Gap a part of West Virginia. That way I could enjoy a stay here and include it in this book. And it is barely in West Virginia. You can actually throw a rock into the Old Dominion from a few of the campsites here. This campground is located in a gap along Old North Mountain, a long, northeast-southwest ridge over which the state line runs. Scenic high-country trails head in both directions through this section of the George Washington National Forest. And what better place to camp than in Wolf Gap, where these trails are but footsteps away?

The campground is located in a transitional forest. Hickory, oak, and dogwood trees, more characteristic of the lower ridges and southern forests, are found here. Also here are birch and cherry, more typical of northern hardwood forests. How appropriate that these trees come together in an area that was literally divided by war between the North and South. There is also some white pine and a steady understory of cherry and maple.

Enter Wolf Gap and turn left into the campground. It is a small loop, which rises away from the gap. The first few sites are flat, but then a little landscaping and leveling had to be done to make the other sites habitable. Campsites #2, #3, and #4

CAMPGROUND RATINGS

Beauty: ★★★
Site privacy: ★★★
Site spaciousness: ★★★★
Quiet: ★★★★★
Security: ★★★
Cleanliness/upkeep: ★★★

Wolf Gap is a rustic campground on the Virginia–West Virginia border. Hike state line trails directly from the campground.

EASTERN PANHANDLE

overlook Virginia. You will probably be gathering firewood in that state.

Most of the sites are on the outside of the loop. The layout has been tastefully done with stone work. You may have to walk up or down a few stone steps to reach your picnic table or tent pad. The sites are average-to-big in size and are well spaced from one another. With only ten sites, you won't feel cramped. It can fill on weekends, but take a chance here. During the week it can get lonely at Wolf Gap. I

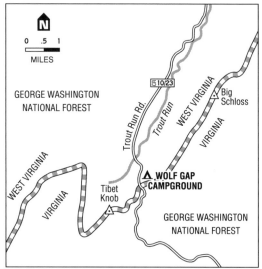

know—I camped here on a Monday by myself. Also, notice there are no trash cans here—this is a "pack it in, pack it out" campground.

Campsites #7 and #8 are the best. They are highest on the hill and are the most spacious and private. Pass the Mill Mountain trailhead, then come to the final two campsites that look toward West Virginia. They also are among the best. In the center of the loop are new-design vault toilets, using SST, a.k.a. Sweet-Smelling Technology. They are an improvement over the hole-in-the-ground-with-a-shed-over-it models of yesteryear. Trust me on this one. Over toward Wolf Gap is an attractive picnic area with a level grassy lawn. The working hand-pump well is over here, but the water was too rusty for me to drink. Bring your own water to be on the safe side. What is a couple of bucks for water when you can camp here for free?

So what about the trails here? On the campground side of the gap, the Mill Mountain Trail heads north. Mill Mountain is a knob on Great North Mountain. But before Mill Mountain is a superb rock lookout called Big Schloss. Head up the Mill Mountain Trail for 2 miles, then take the 0.3-mile trail to the Big Schloss. German settlers on the Virginia side of the mountain called it the Castle. "Schloss" means castle in German. Or maybe it means fantastic lookout into Massanutten Mountain and the Shenandoah Valley in Virginia and also views into West Virginia. This is a must for Wolf Gap campers. You can keep going on the Mill Mountain Trail and come to Sandstone Spring at 4.5 miles. The water is not rusty there.

On the south side of the gap is the Tibbet Knob Trail. It is a shorter but steeper walk to the top of Tibbet Knob. The trail then swings almost north again, following the state line, and heads toward Devils Hole Mountain. More good views can be had from Half Moon Mountain Trail. Drive 5 miles down into West Virginia from Wolf Gap and look for the hiker sign on your right. This is the Half Moon Trail. Cross Trout Run and walk for 2.6 miles to the Half Moon Lookout Trail. Turn left on the Half Moon Lookout Trail and follow it for 0.8 mile to a rock lookout of Trout Run Valley. Get used to it; you'll be looking down on everyone here at Wolf Gap.

To get there: From Wardensville, drive south on Trout Run Road (CR 23/10) for 13.5 miles to Wolf Gap at the state line. The campground will be on your left.

KEY INFORMATION

Wolf Gap Campground
109 Molineau Road
Edinburgh, VA 22834

Operated by: U.S. Forest Service

Information: (540) 984-4101, www.fs.fed.us/gwjnf

Open: Year-round

Individual sites: 10

Each site has: Picnic table, fire ring, lantern post, tent pad

Site assignment: First come, first served; no reservations

Registration: Self-registration on site

Facilities: Pump well, vault toilets

Parking: At campsites only

Fee: None

Elevation: 2,600 feet

Restrictions:

Pets—On leash only

Fires—In fire rings only

Alcoholic beverages—At campsites only

Vehicles—None

Other—14-day stay limit

FEUDIN' COUNTRY

BEECH FORK STATE PARK
Huntington

This is an old-fashioned state park that serves recreators of many stripes from the Huntington area and beyond. Beech Fork combines natural pleasures, such as hiking and nature programs, with organized outdoor activities such as volleyball and basketball. Add water pursuits such as fishing and boating, and mix in a swimming pool and the state park system's largest campground, and you get Beech Fork State Park.

Beech Fork Campground is big, really big. It was built by the Army Corps of Engineers right on the shore of Beech Fork Lake. The setting allows you to enjoy the lake and the hills, which rise out of the watershed. However, the campground itself is on an artificial flat created by the Corps of Engineers.

Pass the park office and come first to the Old Orchard Camping Area. It is open year-round and has water and electrical hookups. The sites are crammed together and look like a parking lot. And it is—for RVs. Do not stay here.

Turn left and cross a bridge over upper Beech Fork, just where the stream flows into the lake. This is the Moxley Branch Camping Area. It has 69 campsites strung out in various loops and spurs. Many campsites are along the lake. The landscape is mainly grass, with some planted trees getting big enough to provide shade. There is one bathhouse and a rest room for

CAMPGROUND RATINGS

Beauty:	★★★
Site privacy:	★★★
Site spaciousness:	★★★★★
Quiet:	★★★★
Security:	★★★★★
Cleanliness/upkeep:	★★★★★

Beech Fork has the largest campground in the state park system. And there is more than the lakeside setting to draw visitors.

FEUDIN' COUNTRY

the loop. These campsites can be reserved, and you might want to reserve a site here on a busy holiday.

Back out on the main road, the Four Coves Camping Area has 88 sites and a bathhouse. Four peninsulas jut out between watery coves that make for an attractive setting. Many trees scattered about are awash in a grassy lawn. Most campsites lie along the water. Many campers pull their boats right up to their campsites.

Pass the boat launch area and come to the final camping

area, the Lakeview Camping Area. Four spur roads end in loops with numerous waterside sites and good views of the lake. There is a bathhouse here, too. Overall, the campground is spread out enough to make it seem smaller than it really is. It is aesthetically pleasing. The campsites are very spacious, but most are a little on the open side, which I personally don't like. So you might as well get friendly with your neighbor here.

At Beech Fork, the campground is not the be all and end all. It is what you do with your time that counts. There are many hiking trails, from the 0.75-mile Nature Trail to the 5-mile Lost Trail that is open to hikers and mountain bikers. The Lakeview Trail passes an old log cabin and pioneer cemetery. The Fitness Trail has exercise stations for those inclined to challenge more than their legs and lungs.

The lake draws many boaters and anglers casting for tiger musky, saugeye, bluegill, catfish, and bass. There is a ten-horsepower motor limit on the lake and many no-wake areas, such as around the campground. Rowboats and paddleboats are rented in summer. The fishing here is good from the bank, too.

This park comes alive in summer. Ranger-led, interpretive programs help you enjoy the natural aspects of the park, and there are also sporting venues for volleyball, tennis, basketball, horseshoes, and baseball or softball.

If it is really hot, you can cool off in the park pool. Swimming is not allowed in the lake. You can check out the game room on a rainy day. Though supplies are available in Huntington, there is a camp store open in the summer. If you can't find anything to do here at Beech Fork State Park, you might as well get back to the couch and flick the remote.

To get there: From I-64 near Huntington, take Exit 11 and head south on WV 10. Follow WV 10 for 1.5 miles to Green Valley Road. Turn right on Green Valley Road and follow it for 7 miles to the state park, which will be on your right.

KEY INFORMATION

Beech Fork State Park
5601 Long Branch Road
Barboursville, WV 25504

Operated by: West Virginia State Parks

Information: (304) 522-0303, www.wvparks.com/beech-fork

Open: Old Orchard Camping Area: year-round; rest of campground: April 15 through October 31

Individual sites: 49 full hookups, 226 electric

Each site has: Picnic table, fire grate

Site assignment: Reservations accepted, but not required

Registration: By phone, or ranger will come by and register you

Facilities: Hot showers, flush toilets, water spigots, coin laundry, camp store in summer

Parking: At campsites only

Fee: $15 per night, full hookup; $13 per night, electric only

Elevation: 600 feet

Restrictions:

Pets—On leash only

Fires—In fire grates only

Alcoholic beverages—Prohibited

Vehicles—None

Other—14-day stay limit

CABWAYLINGO STATE FOREST

Dunlow

The name Cabwaylingo is deceiving. You would think it an Indian name, but it is actually the combination of the counties of which it is a part: Cabell, Wayne, Lincoln, and Mingo. But what's in a name? What is here are two neat campgrounds that offer different experiences and a lot of rugged terrain.

West Virginia saw this as a good candidate for a state forest back in the 1930s, as it was one of the original state forests. During the Great Depression, the Civilian Conservation Corps developed the forest, not too much, but just enough to make it feel homey. Their stone handiwork and the Tick Ridge campground harken back to the old days of camping, when tent camping was the only way to do it. The CCC also built trails that we can walk today.

But there is also a newer side to the Cabwaylingo, such as the pool for hot summer days and the new 11-site Spruce Creek Campground that has many modern features. Built along Spruce Creek, this camping area offers three campsites spread along the creek with water and electricity—which spells RVs. The bathhouse is here. Across the bridge over Spruce Creek are three more RV sites, but off to the right are five tent-only sites that have electricity. Steep ridges give the campground a closed-in feel. Partway up these ridges near the campground entrance are two CCC-built stone shelters that are a real treat to see.

CAMPGROUND RATINGS

Beauty:	★★★★
Site privacy:	★★★
Site spaciousness:	★★★
Quiet:	★★★★
Security:	★★★★★
Cleanliness/upkeep:	★★★★

Campers can enjoy two distinct campgrounds and a lot of natural West Virginia, in a forest that is complemented with the stonework of the Depression-era Civilian Conservation Corps.

FEUDIN' COUNTRY

The other campground, Tick Ridge, is a throwback camp-ground, as in the days of yes-teryear. A gravel road leads from the park's main water-way, Twelvepole Creek, up to the top of Tick Ridge. Just past the road toward Marcum Cemetery is the first camping loop. This loop is in a pine-oak forest with six campsites. All but one campsite are on the inside of the loop. The under-story is minimal and the woods drop off steeply on all sides. The bathhouse and a water spigot are adjacent to

this loop. The grills and a picnic shelter are CCC stonework.

Three campsites continue along the narrow neck of the ridge before it widens out. The final loop is perched on the mountainside, where the only level spots are where you pitch your tent and use your picnic table. All around are great views deep into the forest of oak, tulip trees, and more. Some sites have been allowed to revert to the forest. Pass the Indian Trail, and the spread-out campground continues, with private sites set all along Tick Ridge at dif-ferent elevations and perspectives. Pit toilets and water spigots are conve-niently spread around. It's a safe bet that you will get a campsite here, even on weekends. This campground fills only during major summer holidays.

There are nearly 25 miles of trails to trek here. The Indian Trail leaves the campground and leads a mile down toward the park's group camp. Just a short distance from Tick Ridge is the CCC-built fire tower. You can no longer climb the 1934-era tower itself, but just a few hundred yards of walking takes you from Tick Ridge to obscured views at the tower base. For rock formations, take the Copley Trail. Use the Sleepy Hollow and Martin Ridge Trails for a 3.5-mile partial loop, which you could complete with a bit of road-walking along

Twelvepole Creek. The creek is stocked with trout during the spring months. Watch for the waterfall along Sleepy Hollow Trail.

Near Spruce Creek Campground is the Beech Ridge Trail. Take this trail up to Tick Ridge Road and then loop back down Spruce Creek Trail to the campground. Get a trail map from the park office, then lace up your shoes.

The basketball court can provide a good diversion. You may want to cool off in the park swimming pool, which is open Memorial Day through Labor Day. But, this place is mostly about relaxation and getting back to nature. And that is an important part of any tent-camping experience.

> To get there: From Huntington, drive south on WV 152 for about 42 miles, then turn left on Missouri Branch Road (CR 35) and you'll soon come to the state forest.

KEY INFORMATION

**Cabwaylingo State Forest
Route 1, Box 85
Dunlow, WV 25511**

Operated by: West Virginia State Parks

Information: (304) 385-4255, www.wvparks.com/cab-waylingo

Open: April 15 through October 31

Individual sites: 31

Each site has: Tick Ridge: picnic table, fire grate; Spruce Creek: electricity, water, picnic table, fire grate

Site assignment: First come, first served; no reservations

Registration: Ranger will come by to register you

Facilities: Tick Ridge: showers, water spigots, vault toilets; Spruce Creek: hot showers, flush toilets

Parking: At campsites only

Fee: $ 7 per night, Tick Ridge; $11–15 per night, Spruce Creek

Elevation: Tick Ridge: 1,300 feet; Spruce Creek: 800 feet

Restrictions:

Pets—On leash only

Fires—In fire grates only

Alcoholic beverages— Prohibited

Vehicles—None

Other—14-day stay limit

CHIEF LOGAN STATE PARK

Logan

Southern West Virginia has historically been coal country, with some of the most extensive seams in the United States. Before the arrival of the white man, Mingo Indians called this area home. Chief Logan State Park, the recreational heart of this rich land, is named after the most renowned Mingo, Chief Logan. The parkland was once part of Merrill Coal Company. Now, this area of wooded hills, cut with deep hollows of the Buffalo Creek watershed, is well developed with an eye toward local recreators, yet it keeps true to its past, with historical exhibits and more highlighting the Indian, settler, and coal era of times gone by.

The campground is adequate for the park, which has much to see and do. You can hike its trails, swim in the pool, play on the game courts, go horseback riding, or see the wildlife exhibit. And during parts of the summer, you can see The Aracoma Story, a play about the era when the Mingo first encountered British settlers exploring the continent.

To find the campground, drive past the park restaurant, which serves hungry campers good meals, and turn left along Buffalo Creek. At the head of the hollow is the campground. First, pass many fully-equipped pull-through campsites that attract the big rigs. These line the main road. Cross over Buffalo Creek and more

CAMPGROUND RATINGS

Beauty: ★★★
Site privacy: ★★★
Site spaciousness: ★★★
Quiet: ★★★★
Security: ★★★★★
Cleanliness/upkeep: ★★★★

This state park integrates its historic past with modern facilities.

FEUDIN' COUNTRY

fully-equipped sites continue. The modern bathhouse is on your left.

Finally, arrive at a turn to your right. Veer up the hill to a bench where there are five campsites spoked out from a small loop. These overlook the hollow. Mown grass borders the tables and grates. There is some shade and no RVs.

There is another appealing camping area at the very head of the hollow. There, five sites have paved pull-in areas, as do all the campsites. Some of the sites are in full sun, but

chances are you can get whatever campsite pleases you, because the tent sites never fill here. Most park visitors are locals who just come for the day. This leaves visitors from outside the area to enjoy the camping pleasures along with the park's recreation activities.

Your first order of business is to gain insight into the area's history. From the campground, take the Coal Mine Trail. This path traces an old mine tram road past mine openings and a tipple site. You can also see a coal silo. The trail is a mile long and a good leg stretcher. Next, drive down and look at the pioneer homestead and the locomotive on display. The homestead will make you appreciate modern conveniences. Steam locomotives such as the one here were essential in moving coal from the point of extraction to market.

The natural history of the area can be gained two ways, either on other park trails or at the wildlife exhibit. The wildlife exhibit features native flora and fauna of West Virginia. There are birds, boars, bears, and snakes. Here, you can learn from a park naturalist about the daily existence of local woodland creatures.

Hikers and mountain bikers can explore some of the park's 3,300 acres via 18 miles of trails. The Woodpecker Trail winds up the hollow of Buffalo Creek. The Guyondotte Beauty Trail is great for wildflowers in the spring and also passes more mining ruins. Of special note is the Fitness Trail, which is interspersed with exercise stations along the way.

If you want to be hauled around, take a horseback ride. A stable is located near the campground. They offer guided rides for less-experienced equestrians. Then there's the pool. This watery getaway spells relaxation. Hills rise from either side of the swimming area. The game courts and miniature golf course are located here, too. Playgrounds are scattered throughout the park.

There is a Civil War Reenactment at the park toward the end of September. Summer weekends feature plays put on at the outdoor theater. The Aracoma Story is an annual draw that features the compelling story of a chief's daughter and her ill-fated love of a British soldier. The setting accentuates the story. The setting at Chief Logan State Park will accentuate your tent camping experience, too.

To get there: From the town of Logan, head north on WV 10 for 4 miles. Chief Logan State Park will be on your left.

KEY INFORMATION

Chief Logan State Park
Logan, WV 25601

Operated by: West Virginia State Parks

Information: (304) 792-7125, www.wvparks.com/ chieflogan

Open: March 1 through November 30

Individual sites: 13 electric, 12 nonelectric

Each site has: Picnic table, fire grate

Site assignment: Reservations accepted, but not required

Registration: Ranger will come by to register you

Facilities: Hot showers, flush toilets, water spigot

Parking: At campsites only

Fee: $11 per night tent sites, $17 per night full hookups

Elevation: 1,500 feet

Restrictions:

Pets—On leash only

Fires—In fire grates only

Alcoholic beverages—Prohibited

Vehicles—None

Other—14-day stay limit

KANAWHA STATE FOREST

Charleston

Kanawha State Forest has been under state control for over seven decades. The city of Charleston has spread to Kanawha, and that growth has made the natural world of Kanawha that much more valuable. When you are back here, it is hard to believe the gold capital dome is just a few ridges away. The Davis Creek Camping Area has a rustic aura to it, and some park facilities, built by the Civilian Conservation Corps, add an old-timey touch. But the daily drawing cards are the trails that bring mountain bikers, hikers, and horseback riders to comb the hills and valleys of the Kanawha.

The Davis Creek Camping Area has a different twist to it. Most campgrounds start at the bottom of a valley and work their way up, then turn around. This campground starts at the top of the hollow, works its way down, then turns around.

Enter the upper end of Davis Creek, which is just a small stream at this point, and begin to pass the first campsites to your right. These first sites are rustic and strung along the creek with plenty of distance between them for adequate privacy. They are equipped with only a picnic table and a fire pit made of local stone. One of the first seven campsites is directly creekside. All are adequately level beneath the riparian forest of beech and sycamore, with steep, wooded hills rising from the creek's edge. Look for the hornbeam tree, also known as

CAMPGROUND RATINGS

Beauty:	★★★★
Site privacy:	★★★
Site spaciousness:	★★★
Quiet:	★★★★
Security:	★★★★★
Cleanliness/upkeep:	★★★★★

This mountain getaway is only 7 miles—but feels a world away—from the capital city of Charleston.

FEUDIN' COUNTRY

"musclewood," with its sinewy trunks that resemble a human arm or leg. It grows beside streams and in ravines in mountainous terrain.

Cross a bridge over Davis Creek, and a set of seven rustic campsites are situated on a side hollow and stream. Pass the bathhouse just before you turn left into this hollow. Hemlocks shade some of the campsites, and the smallish valley seems even more intimate.

Back on the main road, a cluster of good tent sites abut Davis Creek. Cross a small

footbridge to get to campsite #21. After this, all the sites are equipped with water and electricity, but ironically, most are less level than the rustic campsites. Below you, on a one-way return road, are four campsites in small flats that are the best and the most private in the campground. Davis Hollow is not big-rig user-friendly. Overall, none of the campsites are too big, but you can find privacy. The campground fills only on the three major summer holidays: Memorial Day, Independence Day, and Labor Day.

Come to the second bathhouse farther down the long hollow and cross yet another bridge. Some sites are along the creek and others are on the hillside. They are well spread apart. The paved road loops around. A short, gravel spur goes a bit farther down the creek and has larger sites designed for trailers under the 30-foot length limit, though I wouldn't want to drive one back this way.

Mountain bikers and hikers love this place! Kanawha is laced with trails that course through over 11,000 acres of preserved terrain. There are even some stands of old-growth forest in Kanawha among the 25-plus miles of trails. You can try out the Store Hollow and Davis Creek Trails from the campground. Mountain bikers really take to the Davis Creek Trail that leaves the lower end of the campground. Take the Overlook Rock Trail for a view and the Hemlock Falls Trail for some water. Many of the trails are hiking only. Stop in the park office and get a good trail map, then set out on your own jaunt.

You may want to ride a horse. The D&M Stables are located right in the forest and offer one- and two-hour trail rides for a fee. A good family activity is their horse-drawn hay ride. The pond near the park entrance, built by the CCC, is stocked with bass and bluegill for anglers. Everyone comes to relax in the campground, but many locals like to recline poolside at the forest swimming pool. Kids love the pool and the playground. There's a little bit for everybody at this woodland getaway in the mountains by the state capital.

To get there: From I-64 in Charleston, take Exit 58A, drive south on U.S. 119. Turn left onto Oakwood Road at the second stoplight. Turn right onto Bridge Road, then right onto Connell Road. At the bottom of Connell Road make a sharp left on Kanawha Forest Drive and follow it to the forest entrance. Brown state forest signs will guide you from U.S. 119.

KEY INFORMATION

Kanawha State Forest
Route 2, Box 285
Charleston, WV 25314

Operated by: West Virginia State Parks

Information: (304) 558-3500, www.wvparks.com/ kanawha

Open: April 15 through October 31

Individual sites: 25 electric, 21 nonelectric

Each site has: Picnic table, fire pit

Site assignment: Reservations accepted, but not required

Registration: By phone, or ranger will come by to register you

Facilities: Hot showers, flush toilets, coin laundry

Parking: At campsites only

Fee: $16 per night for electric sites, $11 per night for non-electric sites

Elevation: 980 feet

Restrictions:

Pets—On leash only

Fires—In fire pits only

Alcoholic beverages— Prohibited

Vehicles—30-foot trailer limit

Other—14-day stay limit

PANTHER STATE FOREST

Iaeger

Panther State Forest is located near the intersection of Virginia, Kentucky, and West Virginia and is the most southerly campground described in this guidebook. This region, steeped in coal-mining culture, is characterized by deep and narrow hollows bottomed with swift creeks and topped with hills rising above. These hills make up in steepness for what they lack in height, compared to more lofty places in the Mountain State. A small, quiet, and never-filled campground is located in one of the few level locales in the forest. From here you can enjoy many of the natural and man-made features that Panther State Forest offers.

The campground is located at the confluence of Panther Creek and Crane Branch in a wooded flat. The six campsites are strung out next to Panther Creek. Overhead, a forest of beech, hemlock, sycamore, and yellow birch provide seasonal shade. The understory is mossy beneath the trees and grassy in adjacent open areas.

Campsite #1 overlooks Crane Branch emptying into Panther Creek. It has an old-fashioned fire pit built of stone and concrete. This campsite is one of the two most popular sites, at a campground that doesn't even fill on July 4! Walk the footbridge over Crane Branch and come to campsite #2. It also has the old-style fire pit. Campsite #3 is the most open. It lies next to a grassy clearing, but is short on flat tent sites.

CAMPGROUND RATINGS

Beauty: ★★★
Site privacy: ★★★★
Site spaciousness: ★★★★★
Quiet: ★★★★
Security: ★★★
Cleanliness/upkeep: ★★★★

Come and visit the hollows and hills of West Virginia's deep south.

FEUDIN' COUNTRY

Campsite #4 is across the grassy clearing but also next to Panther Creek. Campsite #5 was my choice. It has the largest level area and is very close to Panther Creek. Campsite #6 lies beneath a huge beech tree and has disabled access. It is the only campsite that has a paved parking pull-in. This is the most popular campsite of them all.

A vault toilet and hand pump well are located just across the forest road from the intimate campground. But the odd thing about this campground is the electrical outlets for each site. Electrical outlets are very rarely combined with vault toilets and hand pump wells. But no matter here—the electricity will only be to your advantage and will not be much of an attraction to RVs. Or anyone else for that matter. You'll likely have this under-used resource to yourself any day of the week.

I recommend coming in the spring—the wildflowers here are incredible. During my stay the trilliums, among many wildflowers, were really putting on a show. Inquire by phone about bloom times.

Hot showers are available at the bathhouse for the park swimming pool. The pool, along with the children's wading pool, is a big family attraction and is open Memorial Day through Labor Day. A playground is also there for kids to enjoy. There are several fine, developed picnic areas in the forest.

The rest of your activities will be centered around the natural amenities. There are over 7,000 acres in the forest, and the state has recently acquired 15,000 more acres around it. That makes for a lot of room to roam. Those adept with a rod and reel can ply the creeks. The waterways have smallmouth bass year-round and are stocked with trout from March through May. Hikers can leave directly from the campground up the Crane Branch Trail to Buzzard Roost Overlook. Add the Loop Trail to this hike for a 2-mile round trip. The George's Fork Trail also leads to the Buzzard Roost. The Drift Branch Trail leads 1.5 miles to the forest fire tower at 2,100 feet and views into three states. The Twin Rocks Trail breaks off from the Drift Branch Trail and leads along Panther Creek toward the forest group camp.

There are many gas wells in Panther State Forest. What this means for you are over 15 miles of gated roads that offer more terrain to cover, whether you are on foot or a mountain bike. Get a trail map from the forest headquarters before you come, and by all means come. Check ahead for hunting schedules if you plan to do some fall hiking or shooting. Also, acquire all your supplies before you get here, as there are no grocery stores or mega-stores in the vicinity.

To get there: From Iaeger, drive north on U.S. 52 for 1 mile. Turn left on Route 3 at the forest sign to Panther. Continue for 6 miles to the hamlet of Panther. Turn left at the Panther Post Office on CR 3/1, where the road splits into CR 3/2, and follow CR 3/2 3.5 miles to the forest entrance. The campground will be ahead on your right.

KEY INFORMATION

Panther State Forest
Box 287
Panther, WV 24872

Operated by: West Virginia State Parks

Information: (304) 938-2252, www.wvparks.com/panther

Open: April 15 through October 31

Individual sites: 6

Each site has: Picnic table, fire grate, electricity

Site assignment: First come, first served; no reservations

Registration: Ranger will come by to register you

Facilities: Pump well, vault toilet, electricity; showers available Memorial Day through Labor Day

Parking: At campsites only

Fee: $7 per night

Elevation: 985 feet

Restrictions:

Pets—On leash only

Fires—In fire grates only

Alcoholic beverages—Prohibited

Vehicles—None

Other—14-day stay limit

R. D. BAILEY LAKE

Pineville

The Army Corps of Engineers has built many dams across our nation. Most of these have been built for flood control, as is the case at R. D. Bailey Lake. Recreation is secondary and thus has not been promoted. The end result is flood control for the Guyandotte River Valley and a little-used recreation area that is a hidden gem of coal country. The attractive campground is large, and an open campsite is guaranteed. This way you can focus on enjoying the scenic lake tucked away in the mountains of Wyoming and Mingo Counties.

I enjoyed a personal tour of the area by a park staffer. You could sense the pride in his voice as we checked out the facilities. After enjoying the view from the Visitor Center (a must), we drove to the Guyandotte Campground. The entrance road to the campground traces an old railroad grade along the Guyandotte River.

The campground is broken into four sections strung out along the river valley. Each area has its own self-registration station. Cross the old railroad bridge and come to the Reedy Creek area. It has 31 campsites set along an oval loop. The riverside terrain is heavily wooded with thick brush offering campsite privacy. Five campsites offer direct access to the Guyandotte River. All the campsites have paved pull-ins, though some campsites directly by the river do not have electricity. The fully-equipped bathhouse is in the center of the oval.

CAMPGROUND RATINGS

Beauty: ★★★
Site privacy: ★★★★
Site spaciousness: ★★★
Quiet: ★★★★★
Security: ★★★★
Cleanliness/upkeep: ★★★★★

This Army Corps of Engineers lake is one of southern West Virginia's recreational secrets.

FEUDIN' COUNTRY

The Locust Branch area has 62 campsites, 13 of which offer river access. It is the most popular loop. These riverside campsites are heavily wooded and spread far apart. The upper area, set away from the water, is more open and hilly. There are a variety of shaded or open campsites. The camping areas up here are a little on the small side, but have been leveled for ease of setting up your tent. A bathhouse and the campground pay phone are located on this loop.

The Guyandotte River continues its sharp bend. Sugarcamp Branch camping area lies along this curve. Eleven of the 55 sites here are riverside, but are open to the sun and to other campers, due to being placed too close together. These are the least desirable river access sites. The upper area has hillside campsites, some of which are pull-through. There are all varieties of sun and shade, but generally the campsites are a little too close together. This whole area is my last choice.

The Smith Bend area has 17 campsites, none of which access the Guyandotte. A bathhouse and picnic shelter are on this two-way road. Fewer campsites and proximity to the campground boat ramp are this area's best advantages.

Reedy Creek is my favorite camping locale. The Sugarcamp and Smith Bend areas may not be open until the other areas begin to fill. There are always campsites available even on summer holiday weekends. One interesting aspect of the campground is your departure route. It passes through an old railroad tunnel on the way back to the main road.

Each loop has a playground area for kids and horseshoe pits. Cyclists will enjoy the quiet paved roads of the large campground. There are volleyball and basketball courts near the campground boat ramp.

Most recreation, however, centers on the lake. And a scenic lake it is: cliffs line the dammed section of the Guyandotte which makes a serpentine course toward the impressive dam. Swimmers enjoy both the lake and the river. Ski boats and personal watercraft tour the narrow impoundment. If you don't have a boat, they are available at the Guyandotte Point Boat Ramp and Marina. Bank fishermen can easily toss a line in here. Anglers vie for bass, bream, crappie and catfish on the banks or by boat. Solitude seekers can find their own slice of the 630 water acres and 17 miles of shoreline at R. D. Bailey Lake.

The main purpose of the $180 million R. D. Bailey project is flood control; recreation is just not as emphasized. The Guyandotte River used to overflow about every other year. It has been under control since 1980, when the 13-year project was finished. To see this work, start with the view from the Visitor Center, then check out the dam—tours are led by Corps personnel. In the control tower you'll learn what an engineering marvel and life-saving feature a dam actually is. To tour the dam, leave the campground and return to West Virginia 97. Turn right on WV 97 and follow it for 2.2 miles to U.S. 52. Turn right on U.S. 52 and follow for 1.1 miles to the right turn into the Visitor Center.

KEY INFORMATION

R. D. Bailey Lake
P.O. Drawer 70
Justice, WV 24851-0070

Operated by: Army Corps of Engineers

Information: (304) 664-3220

Open: Memorial Day through Labor Day

Individual sites: 168

Each site has: Picnic table, fire grate, most have electricity

Site assignment: First come, first served; no reservations

Registration: Self-registration on site

Facilities: Hot showers, flush toilets, water spigots, pay phone

Parking: At campsites only

Fee: $12 per night

Elevation: 1,040 feet

Restrictions:

Pets—On leash only

Fires—In fire grates only

Alcoholic beverages—Prohibited

Vehicles—None

Other—3 cars and 8 campers per site

To get there: From Pineville, drive west on WV 97 for 18 miles to a paved road where there is a large sign for the Guyandotte Campground. Turn right onto the paved road, pass the guard station, and drive 5.8 miles to the campground.

HEART OF
WEST VIRGINIA

AUDRA STATE PARK

Buckhannon

If I had all the elements of nature at my disposal and I was going to design a campground, I don't know if it would turn out any better than the campground at Audra State Park. Many times a campground will be attractive in most regards, yet will have some flaw that keeps it from being exceptional. This campground has no such flaws. It is exceptional. Why? The place is simply beautiful. Moreover, its design integrates man-made additions into the landscape, and it isn't overdeveloped.

Be forewarned: the campground is the attraction at Audra State Park. As you will see, the park setting is exceptionally scenic, but it is a small state park. What it does offer is A+ scenery: the aquamarine Middle Fork River rushing over rocks, the deep shady woods, thickets of rhododendron, precipitous hillsides littered with boulders. There are a few ways to enjoy this natural splendor here, and there are some attractions in the area, but like others who return to Audra year after year, you come here to camp!

Drop steeply off the main park road and enter the campground, situated in a flat along the Middle Fork River, off to your right. Trees tower overhead. The river noisily cascades in the distance. Make your way past the little-used campground check-in station and you are already seeing why this place is so great. Immense thickets of rhododendron intermingle with large boulders mixed among a dense forest

CAMPGROUND RATINGS

Beauty:	★★★★★
Site privacy:	★★★★★
Site spaciousness:	★★★
Quiet:	★★★★★
Security:	★★★★
Cleanliness/upkeep:	★★★★★

This may be the prettiest campground in the state.

HEART OF WEST VIRGINIA

of hemlock. Campsites are tucked into small clearings that offer maximum camper privacy. On the outside of the loop, campsites lie next to the Middle Fork River. Many directly overlook and access the scenic waterway.

One site has a little footbridge to allow campers closer access to the stream. Small hemlocks fight for sunlight below the taller trees, as the sun shines brightly on the river. The sites on the inside of the loop are even more secluded, to the point that they are overlooked if you are driving faster than 5 mph. However, the first of two bathhouses is fairly easy to spot. A small playground is located by one of the bathhouses. Water spigots are spread throughout the area.

The second half of the campground has more hardwoods and campsites that are a little larger. And more riverside sites are there for the taking. Some sites have small beach areas at the water's edge. As the loop swings away from the Middle Fork, many campsites abut a taller bluff up from the river. Cabin-sized boulders function as campsite barriers. Rhododendron thickets resume. This shrub blooms around late June–early July and is a sight to see. The hillside campsites may not be as level as the riverside sites, but they are as scenic and usually have a leveled tent site.

There is no easy way to get to Audra, and expect a slight risk in securing a campsite. Audra fills on Memorial Day weekend and most weekends in July. Other than that, you should be fine. The park superintendent says the best time to come is September; the weather is still good and Audra begins to show her fall colors.

Audra is named after a town that once stood in the area. Little remains of the community; the area has returned to its natural fairness. They don't even need a swimming pool here. The park just laid out a concrete beach extending into the Middle Fork and used Mother Nature's swimming hole! It is open Memorial Day through Labor Day and has lifeguards on duty and a small snack bar.

Audra was once logged. Loggers built a tram road along the river and this track is now used as the trail to Alum Cave. There is an overhanging bluff here and other scenic overlooks. Continue past Alum Cave and the trail makes a 2.7-mile loop back to the park's picnic area. Another trail, the Rock Cliff Trail, leaves the campground and climbs the bluffs behind the campsites.

Kids like to play in the Middle Fork right at the campground, or tube from the campground downstream to the swimming beach. Spring brings kayakers testing their skills on the Middle Fork from Audra to the confluence with the Tygart Valley River, which then descends into a deep gorge.

Barbour County, home of Audra State Park, has some interesting features itself. Nearby are two historic covered bridges; one was built in 1852, the other in 1856. The town of Philippi, where the first land battle of the Civil War purportedly occurred, is the site of an annual Blue and Gray Reunion in early summer. There's a museum with Civil War memorabilia near the covered bridge in Philippi where you can also get supplies. It may be the only time you want to get away from the campground at Audra State Park.

To get there: From I-79 at Weston, take Exit 99 and follow U.S. 33 east to Talbot Road. Turn left on Talbot Road and follow the signs to the state park.

KEY INFORMATION

Audra State Park
Route 4, Box 564
Buckhannon, WV 26201

Operated by: West Virginia State Parks

Information: (304) 457-1162, www.wvparks.com/audra

Open: Mid-April through mid-October

Individual sites: 65

Each site has: Picnic table, fire grate, moveable wooden bench

Site assignment: First come, first served; no reservations

Registration: Ranger will come by to register you

Facilities: Hot showers, flush toilets, coin laundry

Parking: At campsites only

Fee: $11 per night

Elevation: 1,700 feet

Restrictions:

Pets—On leash only

Fires—In fire grates only

Alcoholic beverages—Prohibited

Vehicles—None

Other—14-day stay limit

BAKERS RUN

Sutton

What makes it worthy? The campground lies along an impounded stretch of the Elk River, which ends up being a snake-like ribbon of still water, merging with the Holly River to make even more ribbons of water, collectively known as Sutton Lake, winding through the mountains. It is about fishing, swimming, and boating—whiling away the warms days of summer by the water.

Drop down into the river bottom where two camping areas are laid out. Pass the campground entrance station and turn right into the first camping area, Mill Creek. This area does not have electric sites. Translation: no RVs. The campsites are laid out in two rows paralleling the shoreline. They are a little on the small side and don't have a whole lot of understory. Shade trees cover most of the campsites along the river.

Fourteen campsites are directly lakeside, and are the most desirable. The row away from the river is less shady and less desirable, though these campsites are closer to the fully-equipped bathhouse and a playground and large field. Water spigots are evenly scattered about the camping area. Five more well-shaded campsites lie along the road as it turns away from the lake. These sites are larger and are some of the first sites occupied in this much less busy, tent camper–friendly loop.

CAMPGROUND RATINGS

Beauty:	★★★
Site privacy:	★★★
Site spaciousness:	★★★
Quiet:	★★★★★
Security:	★★★★★
Cleanliness/upkeep:	★★★★

Bakers Run lies deep in the heart of West Virginia along the mountain-rimmed impoundment of the Elk River.

HEART OF WEST VIRGINIA

Continue down along the Elk River embayment, then come to the Bakers Run camping area on your right. This area is much larger, with 76 campsites. There are five tightly knit rows of electric sites that are so close together they look like an RV dealership. Do not camp here. However, 11 of these campsites are lakeside and will nearly always be taken.

The second half of the camping area is nonelectric and is much less crowded. This section, ironically, has more spacious campsites, though privacy is still minimal due to a lack of understory. Most of these sites are in the open, making for a summertime sun whipping. The saving grace of this area are the six mostly-shaded campsites near the boat ramp. They have fantastic lake views. These campsites will be proudly scoffed up by most tent campers. The Bakers Run bathhouse is on a hill far above the campground.

The boat ramp at Bakers Run is one of your keys to enjoying Sutton Lake. Boating for pleasure is a big draw, with such lake and mountain scenery. You can cruise up the arm of the Holly River and to the marina at Gerald R. Freeman Recreation Area, or head downstream to the Sutton Dam and the Bee Run Recreation Area. Many side creeks also form slender arms for exploring. Most of these side creek embayments are no-wake zones, for minimal intrusion to anglers and divers.

Anglers will be able to cast their line for rainbow trout, walleye, bass, crappie, and catfish. The West Virginia Department of Natural Resources handles the fisheries here at Sutton Lake. If you don't have a boat, you can walk down to the Tunnel Road Fishing Access Area at the far end of Bakers Run.

In the campground, bikers can enjoy the quiet paved roads, though more ambitious riders can tool around on the gravel road that heads up Bakers Run. There is a basketball court and a horseshoe pit for game players. However, you are more likely to find relaxed campers who like to put a little water into their summertime camping adventures here at Sutton Lake.

To get there: From downtown Sutton, head south on old U.S. 19 (CR 19/40) for 4.5 miles to WV 17 (Wolf Creek/Centralia Road). Turn left on WV 17 and follow it for 10 miles to Bakers Run Recreation Area, which will be on your left.

KEY INFORMATION

Bakers Run Recreation Area
P.O. Box 426
Sutton, WV 26601

Operated by: Army Corps of Engineers

Information: (304) 765-2816

Open: Early April through early December

Individual sites: 103 nonelectric, 27 electric

Each site has: Picnic table, fire grate, lantern post

Site assignment: First come, first served; no reservations

Registration: At campground registration booth

Facilities: Hot showers, flush toilets, water spigots

Parking: At campsites only

Fee: $12 per night nonelectric, $14 per night electric

Elevation: 930 feet

Restrictions:

Pets—On leash only

Fires—In fire grates only

Alcoholic beverages—At campsites only

Vehicles—None

Other—14-day stay limit in a 28-day period

BULLTOWN

Flatwoods

The Bulltown area has been busy through the centuries. It was once an Indian stronghold. Later, settlers came in, building a mill on nearby Falls Creek to grind their corn. One of the few passable roads of the 1800s, the Weston and Gauley Turnpike, went through here. This strategic road was the site of a Civil War battle. Today, Bulltown is the site of an Army Corps of Engineers' campground that is adjacent to Burnsville Lake, which backs up a portion of the Little Kanawha River. The Bulltown Historical Area is near the campground and enhances the numerous recreational opportunities provided by the lake, such as boating, skiing, fishing, and swimming. The corps has done a fine job of making the most of this area, lying in the center of the Mountain State.

Truth be known, tent campers will like only some of the campground. There are seven loops and four of them are RV havens. But the first three loops will more than suffice. Pass the check-in station and wind along a road to arrive at Loop A. It has 19 campsites set in a shady hickory-oak forest. It is very hilly, offering vertical relief. The paved pull-ins and tent sites have been leveled, but overall the sites are on the smallish side and a tad close to one another—but they are OK!

Continue just a short distance, passing a fully-equipped bathhouse, and come to Loop B. It shares the bathhouse with

CAMPGROUND RATINGS

Beauty:	★★★★
Site privacy:	★★★
Site spaciousness:	★★★
Quiet:	★★★★
Security:	★★★★★
Cleanliness/upkeep:	★★★★★

Bulltown is set in a historic locale, yet features many modern recreational facilities.

HEART OF WEST VIRGINIA

Loop A. The sites here are much like Loop A, with plenty of shade. Also like Loop A, Loop B has electricity. But the smaller campsites and hilly terrain away from the lake keep out the big rigs.

Beyond this is the Hill Loop. It is situated, as expected, on a hill. It offers a mixture of grass and trees. Some sites are more open than others. Most sites have adequate shade. There is no electricity in these eight sites, nor can they be reserved. Nineteen of the 31 sites on loop A and B can be reserved. Why certain sites were chosen over others to be reserved is a secret known only to the Army Corps of Engineers.

Drive a mile or so farther, then top a hill overlooking the pretty lake and see, ugh!, a sea of RVs down below. There are four camping loops with electricity. They hold a combined 146 big rigs. Stay away from here unless you plan to use the boat ramp, volleyball courts, or horseshoe pit.

Bulltown will fill on most summer weekends, especially holidays. Not surprisingly, Loops A and B are popular because they are so shady. You can enjoy a site here nearly any weekday.

While checking in you noticed the Bulltown Historical Area. It is a great tour. There are old structures that represent West Virginia's past. Most were culled from the land that Burnsville Lake now covers. The staff at the interpretive center will show you around. There are also activities for adults and kids that are held here daily. Inquire about each day's program. Another part of the historical area is the Battle of Bulltown site. Here, you can see Confederate breastworks and Union fortifications, then learn how and why they fought over the covered bridge spanning the Little Kanawha River. Make the walk around the loop at the Confederate Overlook area. Also nearby is the Falls Mill Scenic Area. There was once a grist mill here at the scenic cascade. It is also a good place to bank fish in case you don't have a boat. Boatless campers can also enjoy the nearby swimming beach located on the Little Kanawha arm of the lake.

Boats abound, though, no matter where you are on the 1,000-acre lake. Many of the arms make for scenic boating, so expect to run into them.

Bikers can enjoy the numerous, quiet, paved roads in the large Bulltown area, and hikers can get back to nature on the many trails among the 13,000 land acres. The Whitetail Trail starts near the campground. Obtain a trail map at the campground check-in station and have a good time.

To get there: From Exit 67 on I-79 near Flatwoods, head north on U.S. 19 for 11 miles to Millstone Run Road (CR 19/12). Turn left here and drive for 1 mile to the left turn into the Bulltown Recreation Area. The campground is dead ahead.

KEY INFORMATION

Bulltown Recreation Area
HC 10, Box 24
Burnsville, WV 26335

Operated by: Army Corps of Engineers

Information: (304) 853-2371, reservations (877) 444-6777

Open: C Loop: April 23 through December 5; rest of campground: May 21 through September 7

Individual sites: 196 electric, 8 nonelectric

Each site has: Picnic table, fire grate, lantern post

Site assignment: Reservations accepted, but not required

Registration: At campground registration booth

Facilities: Hot showers, flush toilets, water spigots, pay phone

Parking: At campsites only

Fee: $12 per night nonelectric sites, $14 per night electric sites, $16 per night waterfront electric sites

Elevation: 800 feet

Restrictions:

Pets—On leash only

Fires—In fire grates only

Alcoholic beverages— Prohibited

Vehicles—None

Other—14-day stay limit in 28-day period

CEDAR CREEK STATE PARK

Glenville

If you are looking for a campground that exudes the peaceful side of life, come here. This state park has a scenic campground tucked away in a mountain valley that allows you to set up your tent and while away the hours, appreciating the fact that you have no agenda. Then you can focus on renewing relationships with your fellow campers, whether they be friends or family. And if the folding chair gets a little old, there are many activities here to enjoy that reflect West Virginia's commitment to providing both natural and sporting pursuits.

The campground is situated in the hollow of Big Two Run. Campsites are spread up the creek and allow plenty of privacy and spaciousness. Tent campsites are designated by a "T" before the campsite number. They are scattered throughout the campground. These sites have no electricity and are sometimes smaller than the others. The area is well groomed. Water spigots are spread throughout the campground. Sycamore, white pine, and crab apple trees provide shade. A mown lawn is the primary understory.

Pass the camp office, located in an authentic log cabin that was moved to the site from Glenville. Campers register here; the park staff is available to answer camper questions. Ahead on your left is the group campground, designated by the "B" campsites, which are used as overflow. The campground generally fills up the three

CAMPGROUND RATINGS

Beauty:	★★★★
Site privacy:	★★★
Site spaciousness:	★★★★
Quiet:	★★★★
Security:	★★★★★
Cleanliness/upkeep:	★★★★★

Located in the heart of West Virginia, this family-oriented, peaceful getaway is used time and again by campers.

HEART OF WEST VIRGINIA

major holidays and some weekends in summer.

Come to the regular campsites located on both sides of the road, passing the first of three bathhouses. Having three bathhouses in a 47-site campground nearly assures you of no wait when clean-up time comes around. There is a small playground here, too. The campsites near the first bathhouse have the least shade. Campsite #7 is up a side hollow and is also a trailhead for the Stone Trough Trail.

Cross over Two Run and

note some sites on the flat by the creek and some other sites on the hill away from the creek. Cross the creek again, and the sites are on the road, left, near the second bathhouse. More dispersed sites continue, with some sites that are pull-through. The hollow opens up one final time as a side creek comes in from the right. This creates a wide flat where the last sites at the head of the hollow lie beneath oak and buckeye trees. Here is the third and newest bathhouse. The road turns around. There is one campsite in the center of the turnarounds, and it is the only campsite at Cedar Creek I would not like to stay in.

When you decide to get out of the folding chair, you may want to enjoy a cultural pursuit first. On your way to the campground you undoubtedly noticed the white building on a hill to the left. This is an authentic, one-room schoolhouse that has been restored and furnished as if the class has gone to lunch on a school day in the 1920s. A park naturalist leads groups through the schoolhouse on Saturdays in the summer.

The swimming pool is a big draw here. It is open Memorial Day through Labor Day. If you are feeling competitive, try the tennis courts or miniature golf, or you may want to fish. There are three ponds covering ten acres in which you can cast a line. Trout are stocked in spring, and bass, crappie, catfish, and bluegill can be caught year-round. Don't forget the park's namesake, Cedar Creek. Bass are in there and so are canoes with fishermen angling for them. The canoes could also be filled with campers enjoying the beauty of the creek when the water is high enough to float a canoe. Bring your own canoe. The park does rent paddle boats to tool around the fishing ponds.

West Virginia State Parks are known for hiking and Cedar Creek is no exception. The most popular trails are the Stone Trough and the Park View Trails. The Stone Trough Trail leaves the campground and makes a 2.5-mile loop, which passes a stone watering trough, hand-carved from solid rock over a century ago. The Park View Trail is a challenging 2 miles and passes a rock outcrop, affording views of your natural setting. Add the Cedar Creek Trail to make a loop or if you want to fish from the banks of Cedar Creek. The Two Run Trail follows Two Run up to its source and ties in to the Stone Trough Trail.

The ultimate testimony to a good campground is when campers return year after year. While inquiring about the campground, that was one of the first things park personnel brought up. I knew then that Cedar Creek was a winner.

To get there: From Glenville, drive south on U.S. 19 for 4 miles, then turn left on Cedar Creek Road (CR 17) and follow it for 4 miles to the state park, which will be on your right.

KEY INFORMATION

Cedar Creek State Park
Route 1, Box 9
Glenville, WV 26351

Operated by: West Virginia State Parks

Information: (304) 462-7158, www.wvparks.com/cedar-creek

Open: Mid-April through mid-October

Individual sites: 12 nonelectric, 35 electric

Each site has: Picnic table, fire grate

Site assignment: First come, first served unless reserved

Registration: By phone or at campground cabin

Facilities: Hot showers, flush toilets, phone, laundry

Parking: At campsites only

Fee: $11 per night nonelectric, $16 per night electric

Elevation: 750 feet

Restrictions:

Pets—On leash only

Fires—In fire grates only

Alcoholic beverages—Prohibited

Vehicles—None

Other—14-day stay limit

COOPERS ROCK STATE FOREST

Morgantown

Coopers Rock is the largest state forest in West Virginia. And it is probably the most studied as well. A good portion of this wooded mountain land is a part of the West Virginia University Forest, which exercises forestry techniques and their impacts on the land and all that grows on it. That is fitting for the flagship state university, which is but a few miles away. While camping here, check out not only the natural beauty, but head into Morgantown for a taste of university life, West Virginia style.

Coopers Rock is named for a barrel maker, a cooper, who lived on the mountain in the old days. The rock is an outcropping that overlooks the Cheat River Gorge. This area was once the center of the iron industry in the United States. The Henry Clay Iron Furnace, in the state forest, is a well-preserved example of the iron-making technology of the early 1800s. The timber of the area was used to fire the furnaces. Later, nearly the whole area was logged for wood products. The land has been recovering ever since the state took it over in 1936.

The 25-site McCollum Campground was added in the 1960s. It is situated on the east side of the main ridge. Even though it is on the side of the ridge, there are many level campsites. The well-wooded camping area with a mostly grassy understory is high quality. You won't find a bad campsite in the entire place.

CAMPGROUND RATINGS

Beauty: ★★★★
Site privacy: ★★★
Site spaciousness: ★★★★
Quiet: ★★★★
Security: ★★★★★
Cleanliness/upkeep: ★★★★★

Camp in the impressive and historic high country near Morgantown, site of West Virginia University.

HEART OF WEST VIRGINIA

Begin the teardrop-shaped loop and take the paved high road, passing three campsites; then pass the campground check-in station and heated bathhouse. This makes showering much more pleasant on those nippy mornings. Then the campground splits into two 11-site loops. The outer loop has more naturally level campsites, which have gravel pull-ins. Hemlocks are interspersed throughout the hardwood forest. The campsites face out to the deep woods, where you can see boulders that have tumbled down from the higher ridge.

The campsites on the inner loop have been leveled. The well-shaded sites boast added privacy, due to the site-leveling that's held fast by wooden borders. A couple of pull-through sites will draw RVs. There are good views of the rocky hillside. At a glance, campers will notice McCollum Campground is well kept and well maintained, even though from late May through August the campground will fill nearly every weekend. Reservations are accepted only from the Friday before Memorial Day through Labor Day. Also, it will fill when the West Virginia Mountaineers are playing home football games in the fall.

So what is the draw? Rock climbing is big here. And there are plenty of rock outcroppings, as evidenced by the park's namesake, Coopers Rock, which is easily accessible by a short trail. Other overlooks are at Rock City, whose access trail also starts near Coopers Rock, and Raven Rock, which you can reach by foot from the campground. Another good view can be had from the Sand Springs Fire Tower.

Other trails among the 45 miles of pathways here are over in the University Forest side of the state forest. The Virgin Hemlock Trail passes through a stand of old-growth hemlock trees estimated to be 300 years old. Get some exercise and a history lesson on the Clay Run Trail. It starts at the campground entrance and goes down 2.5 miles to the historic Henry Clay Iron Furnace. Imagine the bustling scenes here 150 years ago, with the furnace going, men bringing in hand-dug ore, limestone and hand-cut timber. There were once over 100 log houses in the vicinity and 200 men employed during the furnace's 12-year run.

There are many other trails. Stop at the Forest Headquarters and get a trail map.

If you want to fish, a six-acre trout pond is stocked in spring and during October. And if you need a change from the wildlife of the forest, check out the wild life in Morgantown. University towns are always worth a visit, and this one is no exception.

To get there: From Morgantown, take I-68 east to Exit 15, then turn right into the state forest and follow the forest road for 1.6 miles to McCollum Campground, which will be on your left.

KEY INFORMATION

Coopers Rock State Forest
Route 1, Box 270
Bruceton Mills, WV 26525

Operated by: West Virginia State Parks

Information: (304) 594-1561, www.wvparks.com/coopersrock

Open: April 1 through December 15

Individual sites: 25

Each site has: Electricity, picnic table, fire grate, lantern post

Site assignment: Reservations accepted, but not required

Registration: By phone or at campground check-in station

Facilities: Hot showers, flush toilets, water spigots, pay phone

Parking: At campsites only

Fee: $16 per night

Elevation: 2,070 feet

Restrictions:

  Pets—On leash only

  Fires—In fire grates only

  Alcoholic beverages—Prohibited

  Vehicles—None

  Other—14-day stay limit

HOLLY RIVER STATE PARK

Hacker Valley

CAMPGROUND RATINGS

Beauty:	★★★
Site privacy:	★★★
Site spaciousness:	★★★
Quiet:	★★★★
Security:	★★★★★
Cleanliness/upkeep:	★★★★

Many waterfalls and man-made facilities attract campers to the longest campground around.

Webster County is one of the more remote, hilly sections of the state, and that's saying a lot. Holly River State Park is a preserved slice of the county's finest scenery. These hills were carved over time by precipitation. The heavy rainfall this part of the state receives results in the dramatic waterfalls for which Holly River State Park is known. Trails lead to the falls and many other natural features of the land.

Beyond the trail system are game courts, a swimming pool, and nature programs. What Holly River should also be known for is having one of the longest campgrounds in the state. Over 80 campsites are stretched alongside Laurel Fork, before the waterway merges with Left Fork Holly River. The long camping area has fair, good, and great campsites. This in one place where you must scout the camping area and pick the campsite that suits you. Warning—there will be some RVs scattered in the mix of campsites.

Turn into the paved campground road with gravel spur pull-ins. Every campsite has electricity. The first section has campsites that are a little close to the main road. The oak, hickory, maple, and tulip tree forest has a light understory. Head on down to the next section. Some campsites lie next to a steep hill to your left and are little less than level. After that are many campsites strung right along Laurel Fork. These well-shaded sites have a little rhododendron for

HEART OF WEST VIRGINIA

added privacy. Continue a good way down the road, where families will be pedaling bikes together, and come to another camping area. A thick hemlock woodland provides year-round shade. The creek is bigger down here, with many campsites along it. Other sites lie across the road, adjacent to the mountainside. In this area, as in other areas of this campground, are great campsites right alongside the less-than-great ones. The inside of the loop here is less popular.

To Buckhannon

Laurel Fork

HOLLY RIVER
STATE PARK

Left Fork Holly River

0 .5 1
MILES

More camping areas, with conveniently placed bathhouses, continue. The final camping area has more pines and bigger campsites. In the whole campground, there are only 27 campsites that can be reserved. You should get a reservation before big holidays and on weekends in high summer if you are coming from afar. However, it is also a decent idea to actually pick out your campsite in person if you can, due to the wide variety of desirable and less-than-desirable campsites.

Once here, go waterfall-bagging. There are four major waterfalls at Holly River State Park. You can head to Tecumseh Falls on the Reverie Trail, or Tenskwatawa Falls on a spur trail from the Wilderness Trail. Other paths of the 35 miles of trails lead past old homesites and good views. The Potato Knob Trail goes to the Upper Falls and down to the Chute. It also leads up to a large rock outcrop with great views. The Nature Rock Garden Trail is a shorter interpretive trail that has many wildflowers in season. Get a trail map at the park office. Try to see all the falls and also climb Potato Knob. It will give you a good idea why all this surrounding vertical ground has so much falling water.

After you are finished with the falls, take a dip in the park pool, which is open Memorial Day through Labor Day. You and your group can also get into a little organized sports competition on the volleyball, basketball, or tennis courts. A park naturalist hosts programs during the summer. Biking the park roads is very popular, too.

Sometimes when tent camping, a cookout is a chore. At Holly River you can eat at the park restaurant. This can be handy, as Webster Springs involves a winding drive for its eateries. Full-service stores are located there, should you need to make a supply run. Buckhannon is a good haul to the north. Try to stay put once at Holly River and make the most of your precious tent-camping times.

To get there: From Buckhannon, drive south on WV 20 for 32 miles. Holly River State Park will be on your left.

Holly River State Park
P.O. Box 70
Hacker Valley, WV 26222

Operated by: West Virginia State Parks

Information: (304) 493-6353, www.hollyriver.com

Open: April 15 through October 31

Individual sites: 88

Each site has: Picnic table, fire grate, electricity

Site assignment: Reservations accepted, but not required

Registration: By phone or at campground check-in station

Facilities: Hot showers, flush toilets, water spigots, coin laundry

Parking: At campsites only

Fee: $16 per night

Elevation: 1,800 feet

Restrictions:

*Pets—*On leash only

*Fires—*In fire grates only

*Alcoholic beverages—*Prohibited

*Vehicles—*None

*Other—*14-day stay limit

PLEASANT CREEK WILDLIFE MANAGEMENT AREA

Philippi

This place should be named Pleasant Campground. Meandering along a ridge, this camping area is laid out with good sites in mind and no worries about cramming too many campers in too little area. Tygart Lake, an Army Corps of Engineers impoundment, is just a half mile away. There is good hiking, fishing, and wildlife viewing in the Wildlife Management Area. The more developed facilities of Tygart Lake State Park are just a boat ride or short drive away from Pleasant Creek. The campground at Tygart Lake has too many big rigs for me. And the campsites are too hilly. Don't ask me why all the RVs end up there. Plus, Pleasant Creek is a lot cheaper!

Drive down the valley of Pleasant Creek and pass an arm of the lake before entering the campground. Register at the check-in station and pick a campsite. Immediately off to your right is a loop with five spacious sites, a grassy yard with a playground in the center, and a forested perimeter. The first campsite has a covered roof over its picnic table. These campsites aren't overly private, but are good for families with kids.

To your left is a spur road with 13 ultra-spacious campsites. Several sites offer disabled access. The spur road runs along a ridge and is well shaded beneath an oak-hickory forest. The understory consists of smaller trees and brush. Good views of the woods below the ridge add to the camp-

CAMPGROUND RATINGS

Beauty: ★★★★
Site privacy: ★★★★
Site spaciousness: ★★★★
Quiet: ★★★★
Security: ★★★★
Cleanliness/upkeep: ★★★★

Pleasant Creek is the campground of choice for tent campers on Tygart Lake. Enjoy this area and Tygart State Park across the water, too.

HEART OF WEST VIRGINIA

sites here. A pump well and vault toilet are close by. The road ends in a small loop, with a few campsites on the outside of the loop.

The main campground road goes straight ahead from the check-in station and turns right, passing a few secluded sites on the left. More sites overlook a hollow to the right. The road then meanders up a hill, passing another pump well and bathroom area. Campsites are well dispersed, well maintained, and nearly every site lures you to pull your vehicle in. It fills on major holiday weekends during the summer. Other than that, campsites should be available.

There are hiking and fishing opportunities here at Pleasant Creek. The Lake Trail leaves the campground from the end of the center spur road and heads down and around the lake. There are many other unnamed trails that thread the area. Obtain a brochure at the area office. Near the campground is a boat launch. The dam-like structure you may see in the water is a waterfowl impoundment. Boaters can angle from the lake for warm water species. Even if you don't have a boat, you can bank fish, as I saw many campers do during my visit.

If you want to go to Tygart Lake State Park, head back out to U.S. 119 and turn right (north) and drive 6 miles into Grafton. While there, pay a visit to the Grafton National Cemetery, where Civil War veterans are buried. Once at Grafton, follow the signs 3 miles to the state park. You will also pass the visitor center at the Tygart Lake dam, run by the Army Corps of Engineers. Inside are interesting displays about the dam, how it was made, and what it does. The Tygart Dam Trail leaves here, passes by the dam and the park lodge before looping around to intersect the Dogwood Trail and returning to the visitor center. The state park has other trails as well. A park naturalist offers programs during the summer.

A full-scale marina on the lake welcomes boaters and offers boat rentals. Water skiers, anglers, and even scuba divers will be found on the clear impoundment. There is also a lakeside swimming area with a grassy lawn for sunbathing and game courts. Indulge in these developed facilities, then return to the rustic and pleasant campground across the lake at Pleasant Creek.

To get there: From Philippi, head north on U.S. 119 for 6 miles and come to Pleasant Creek at the Barbour-Taylor county line. Turn right at the sign for Pleasant Creek, soon pass under a high train trestle and come to the campground after 3 miles.

KEY INFORMATION

Pleasant Creek WMA
Route 3, Box 180
Philippi, WV 26416

Operated by: Division of Natural Resources

Information: (304) 457-5144, www.dnr.state.wv.us

Open: Year-round

Individual sites: 40

Each site has: Picnic table, fire grate, lantern post

Site assignment: First come, first served; no reservations

Registration: Self-registration on site

Facilities: Pump well, vault toilets

Parking: At campsites only

Fee: $5 per night

Elevation: 1,100 feet

Restrictions:

Pets—On leash only

Fires—In fire grates only

Alcoholic beverages—Prohibited

Vehicles—None

Other—14-day stay limit

NEW RIVER VALLEY

ARMY CAMP

Beckley

A name like Army Camp leads you to believe this location has been camped on for some time. During World War II, the Army Corps of Engineers built bridges over the New River for training. Many of the corps members were probably here against their will, but you will find no one of that sentiment today, for Army Camp is a fine campground run by the National Park Service. It was remodeled and opened for business in spring of 1999. From here, the trails of Glades Creek, the restored railroad town of Thurmond with its trails, and the water pursuits of the New River are all nearby. Throw in a little auto touring and you have a great outing in hand.

Army Camp, also known as Camp Prince, is set on a hairpin bend in the New River. First the waterway heads west, then north, and finally back east, before resuming its northern course. All around you, the walls of the river gorge rise high overhead. The white noise of McCreery Rapid bubbles continuously in the distance.

The campground is laid out in a loop. The center is mostly clear, as it once was when this locale was farmland. Pass the day-use area on your right and immediately come to the bathroom building. The first campsite is on the inside of the loop and is shaded by a lone tree. A river access trail leads right to the New. The rest of the riverbank is wooded. The second of five campsites on the inside of the loop comes next.

CAMPGROUND RATINGS

Beauty: ★★★★
Site privacy: ★★★
Site spaciousness: ★★★★
Quiet: ★★★★
Security: ★★★★
Cleanliness/upkeep: ★★★★

The water, land, and history of the New River Gorge await you here.

NEW RIVER VALLEY

Pass a second river access trail on your right, then come to four nicely wooded camp-sites on the outside of the loop. These offer views of the gorge, yet are well shaded. These sites, like all the others, have excellent tent pads of wood chips. These wood chips allow stakes to be easily driven into them, adequate drainage, and make for soft ground and a better night's sleep.

On my stay at Army Camp, a summer storm rolled through. I hurriedly put up my tent as lightning was illuminating the sky in the distance. The tent stakes held fast while the wind whipped and buckets of rain dropped from overhead. I stayed completely dry while thunderclaps echoed through the canyon, creating an impressive yet ominous sound.

Pass two more wooded sites on the outside of the loop. The wooded sites generally are occupied first, though boaters prefer the campsites closest to the water. During the warm months, Army Camp will fill on weekends. Other than that you should have no trouble getting a campsite, even though they are free.

Around Army Camp you can fish the river. The New is one of the best warm water fisheries in the state. Smallmouth bass and catfish are angler favorites. A trail leaves the day-use area and follows the river before turning up to McKendree Road. Turn right on the gravel McKendree Road and return to the bridge near Army Camp to make a loop.

McKendree Road is great for auto touring. From Army Camp it is an approximately 45-minute scenic drive to the old railroad town of Thurmond. A park visitor center occupies the restored train depot. From here, you can tour the old town by foot and learn more about life in the New River Gorge during the early 1900s, when coal fueled explosive growth in West Virginia.

There are several trails in the Thurmond area for hikers and bikers. The Thurmond-Minden Trail follows an old railroad grade along the river, where you cross over five trestles offering great views into the gorge, and of Thurmond. The Stone Cliff Trail follows the New River upstream and leads to the Bragg Homestead Site. The Brooklyn–Southside Junction Trail goes through some abandoned mining towns.

And what is a trip to the New River without getting on the river? The section between Hinton and Thurmond is suitable for canoes and kayaks, offering class I–III water. Below Thurmond to the New River Gorge Bridge is big water with rapids ranging from class III–V. The rapids are huge here and ideal for rafting. Numerous outfitters operate in the area. Dial (800) Call-WVA for a list of licensed outfitters.

After all the fun here, you will find yourself leaving Army Camp against your will.

To get there: From Beckley, take WV 41 north for 9 miles toward Prince. Cross the bridge over the New River, then take your first left. The left turn is just after the bridge crossing. Follow this road for 2 miles and dead-end at Army Camp.

KEY INFORMATION

Army Camp
P.O. Box 246
Glen Jean, WV 25846

Operated by: National Park Service

Information: (304) 465-0508, www.nps.gov/neri

Open: Year-round

Individual sites: 11

Each site has: Picnic table, fire grate, lantern post, tent pad

Site assignment: First come, first served; no reservations

Registration: Ranger will come by to register you

Facilities: Vault toilet (bring water)

Parking: At campsites only

Fee: None

Elevation: 1,200 feet

Restrictions:

   Pets—On leash only

   Fires—In fire grates only

   Alcoholic beverages—At campsites only

   Vehicles—None

   Other—14-day stay limit in 28-day period

BABCOCK STATE PARK

Clifftop

Babcock is one of West Virginia's first state parks. It was inaugurated July 1, 1937. The allure of this part of the Appalachian Plateau made it a logical choice. The Civilian Conservation Corps developed the park, and later other amenities were added. The state was right in picking this locale, but little did they know that another primary attraction would develop very nearby. This attraction is the rafting on the lower New River Gorge. Some of the most exciting and certainly most scenic rafting in the country is on the New River. Babcock abuts the New River Gorge National River. Not only can you enjoy the facilities and beauty of Babcock, but also hook up with a commercial outfitter from Fayetteville and take on the wild rapids of the New.

The campground has potential, but I question the location. It is set 2 miles from the main noncamping facilities in the park and is split in two by a road. Granted, the road is little used, but with all the pretty terrain, why put it where it is? Anyway, the site is on a piece of forested plateau land. The main camping area can only be described as an agglomeration of small loops that stay on the most level part of the plateau.

Beyond the check-in station is a hemlock, white pine, oak, and hickory forest. Pass a few sites under shady hemlocks, then come to a more open area where oak and hickory

CAMPGROUND RATINGS

Beauty:	★★★
Site privacy:	★★★
Site spaciousness:	★★★★
Quiet:	★★★
Security:	★★★★
Cleanliness/upkeep:	★★★★

Stay at Babcock and raft the wild rapids of the lower New River Gorge.

NEW RIVER VALLEY

dominate overhead. The campsites are normal in size, but privacy is lacking due to the light understory. The second small loop has electric campsites and a bathhouse.

Other sites here are erratically arranged on islands inside gravel roads. The sites are passable, just a little on the open side. Across the road are campsites numbered 41–51. The paved loop is centered in a field with a periphery of woodland. All the sites are on the outside of the loop, allowing shade at some camping spots. Others are wide open. These electric sites are for the big rigs. Stay on the other side of the road.

This campground fills just about every weekend during the summer and is busy all of July. It is also busy during the fall rafting season on the Gauley River, another nearby waterway with very exciting rafting. Reserve a site if you are coming from a long way during these periods.

The main draw here is rafting, but the park itself should not be overlooked. There are around 20 miles of hiking and mountain biking trails. Mountain bikes are available for rent during the summer. The Old Sewell Road leads down to the New River, where you can check out the waters. You can bike a 12-mile loop by using Old State Road and Old Sewell Road. Hikers can head to scenic overlooks on the Island-in-the-Sky Trail. Manns Creek Gorge Trail also offers views. There is a stable near the campground that offers guided horseback rides for adults and pony rides for kids.

You may wish to tour the Old Mill down on Glade Creek. It is a reconstructed structure using pieces of other authentic mills from around the state.

Meal is actually ground there today. There are daily tours in the summer and on weekends during the spring and fall.

Boley Lake has 19 acres of fishing. You can also rent paddleboats, rowboats, and canoes. Jump in the swimming pool if you feel like getting wet. There are game courts on site, and a park naturalist holds programs during the summer.

But what most folks come for is the rafting. Rapids range up to Class V, which means go with a guided outfit for a fun and safe outing. The section of river from Thurmond down to the famous New River Gorge bridge is challenging. From the Sewell area down to the bridge has the most rapids, with names like Millers Folly and Double Z. For a list of licensed outfitters, call (800) 927-0263 or visit www.newrivercvb.com on the Web. I have been down the New during the fall color season and found it to be one of my favorite outdoor adventures in West Virginia. Your trip will be noteworthy no matter when you go.

To get there: From Fayetteville, drive north on U.S. 19 to U.S. 60. Head east on U.S. 60 for 10 miles to WV 41 South. Head south on WV 41 for 2 miles and turn right on Clifftop Road. Follow Clifftop Road a short distance to the campground. The registration building will be on your left.

KEY INFORMATION

Babcock State Park
HC 35, Box 150
Clifftop, WV 25831

Operated by: West Virginia State Parks

Information: (304) 438-3004, www.babcocksp.com

Open: Mid-April through October 31

Individual sites: 28 electric, 24 nonelectric

Each site has: Picnic table, fire grate

Site assignment: First come, first served unless reserved

Registration: By phone or at campground registration station

Facilities: Hot showers, flush toilets, water spigot, coin laundry, pay phone, soda machine

Parking: At campsites only

Fee: $16 per night electric, $11 per night nonelectric

Elevation: 2,700 feet

Restrictions:

Pets—On leash only

Fires—In fire rings only

Alcoholic beverages— Prohibited

Vehicles—None

Other—14-day stay limit

BLUESTONE STATE PARK

Hinton

The 2,000-acre Bluestone Lake is the focal point of this state park. It is the impoundment of the New and Bluestone Rivers, creating ribbons of water amid steep hollows cut into the land. The free-flowing section of the Bluestone River, above the lake, is a federally designated wild and scenic river. The nearby southern end of the New River Gorge National River offers a couple of good waterfalls for your viewing pleasure. The state park has been developed on the rugged shores of the lake, making for a good place to camp awhile.

Boating and fishing are the top draws, but the hills and hollows make for challenging hiking, with an accent on spring wildflowers and fall colors. A pool, a recreation building with lots of equipment for games, and other man-made amenities keep you busy. So do summer, nature, and park programs.

The campgrounds barely make the grade in comparison to the natural beauty of the area. Meador Campground is more developed and in better shape, but the development attracts the RV crowd. It does have an eight-site tent area that is OK. Old Mill Campground has potential, but could be better developed as a great tent campground. But it is cheap by state park standards.

The Meador Campground is laid out in a rough figure eight along the shore of Bluestone Lake. Much of it is open, but

CAMPGROUND RATINGS

Beauty:	★★
Site privacy:	★★
Site spaciousness:	★★★
Quiet:	★★★★
Security:	★★★★★
Cleanliness/upkeep:	★★★★★

Bluestone Lake was designed for flood control but is now a recreational haven for water lovers.

NEW RIVER VALLEY

there are decent pockets of white pine, cedar, sycamore, and locust. Drop down on the outer loop and pass along the lake. Six of the campsites are lakeside. Tent campers should be interested in sites #12, #13, and #14. They do not have electricity and are right on the lake. Swing back up the hill and hit the inner loop. The roads are paved and so are the pull-ins. All the well-dispersed campsites here have electricity. The whole set-up spells RV.

Nearby is the eight-site tent camper area. It is a shady pine grove on a knoll. The slightly sloped sites spoke downhill away from the top of the knoll. There are rock fire rings and picnic tables at the bunched-together campsites. There is a bathroom here, but hot showers are available at Meador Campground.

The Old Mill Campground is set on its own in a flat by the Bluestone River. The campsites are in grassy areas alongside the lake. The sites have just a rock fire ring and a picnic table. The sites near the boat launch are in the open, save for the ring of woodland around the grassy center, where tenters camp. Once you get past campsite #20, the river birch woodland increases and shade becomes more abundant. There are 23 riverfront sites.

Make the loop on the gravel road at Old Mill and climb a hill, where the campsites are much more wooded. With a little leveling, these could be great tent sites. Be sure to keep your head on the uphill side of the slope when you try to sleep. The best tent sites are around campsite #37. There is a bathhouse with cold showers for Old Mill campers.

Each of the three camping areas has its pluses and minuses. You will just have to come here and weigh them for yourself. Meador fills on holidays and summer weekends. But you can almost always get a site at Old Mill or the tent area.

By the time you have found a campsite, you will have realized what rugged and beautiful country this is. Most folks enjoy the views from the lake looking up. If you didn't bring your boat, there are boats and canoes for rent at the park marina.

The park pool isn't nearly as big as Bluestone Lake, but it is a good place to cool off. It is located next to Meador Campground. You can play croquet or shuffleboard by renting equipment at the recreation building. Look for posted activities led by park personnel. A park naturalist leads programs daily Memorial Day through Labor Day.

The naturalist may coax you onto some park trails. You can trace the former Kanawha Turnpike, a road designated by the old Virginia Assembly in 1838. It was the equivalent of I-77 in those days. This trail lasts a mile and offers lookouts into the mountains. The Overlook Trail also offers vistas. You can take the Big Pine Trail from the Old Mill Campground to connect to these and other pathways.

If you haven't had enough water, drive north on West Virginia 20 to Hinton (where supplies are available) and continue on the west bank of the New River on River Road to check out Brooks Falls and Sandstone Falls. These are major rapids on the New River Gorge National River. It will give you an idea what cut all these deep hollows around Bluestone.

KEY INFORMATION

Bluestone State Park
HC 78, Box 3
Hinton, WV 25951

Operated by: West Virginia State Parks

Information: (304) 466-2805

Open: Meador: late April through October 31; Old Mill: Memorial Day through Labor Day

Individual sites: 65 nonelectric, 22 electric

Each site has: Meador: Picnic table, fire grate, lantern post; Old Mill: picnic table, fire ring

Site assignment: Reservations accepted, but not required

Registration: By phone or at park office

Facilities: Hot showers, cold showers, flush toilets

Parking: At campsites only

Fee: Meador: $16 per night electric, $11 per night nonelectric; Old Mill: $8 per night

Elevation: 2,000 feet

Restrictions:

Pets—On leash only

Fires—In fire rings only

Alcoholic beverages—Prohibited

Vehicles—None

Other—14-day stay limit

To get there: From Hinton, drive south on WV 20 for 5 miles to Bluestone Park Road (CR 20/2). Turn right on Bluestone Park Road and enter the park.

CAMP CREEK STATE PARK AND FOREST

Camp Creek

Camp Creek State Park and Forest is 5,000 acres of southern West Virginia that is often passed by for other, better-known attractions in the area. Some visitors camp here because it is 2 miles off I-77. There is no doubt that it is a good place to stop on the way to somewhere else, yet it is a worthy destination in its own right. The state park has adequate facilities to keep any tent camper happy. The state forest offers glimpses into a changing landscape that was once farms but is now scientifically managed for wildlife and timber enhancement. Many old roads, now gated, provide mountain bikers and hikers with a chance to enjoy this forest. The Blue Jay Campground, near Campbell Falls, is a shady retreat any tenter would proudly call home.

There are actually two campgrounds here: Mash Fork and Blue Jay. The state forest was established in 1953, and the state park culled from the forest in 1987. After the park was established, the state saw the need for a more-developed, RV-oriented campground, and Mash Fork was born. Tent campers need not bother staying here. Just know that hot showers are available for you here if you are staying at Blue Jay Campground, which is a mile away.

Drive past the park picnic area and come to Blue Jay. It is situated beside gurgling Camp Creek. All 12 campsites lie directly along the waterway, beneath a shade-rendering hemlock forest, accented with

CAMPGROUND RATINGS

Beauty: ★★★
Site privacy: ★★★
Site spaciousness: ★★★
Quiet: ★★★★
Security: ★★★★★
Cleanliness/upkeep: ★★★★

If you are traveling down I-77 and need a place to stop, Camp Creek is convenient. But you may find yourself staying a few days and getting off schedule.

NEW RIVER VALLEY

ironwood. Ironwood is also known as American hornbeam or "musclewood" because the gray bark of the tree resembles the sinewy muscles of a human arm or leg. Pioneers, like those who lived in the area before it became a state forest, used this heavy, tough wood for handles, levers, wedges, or land sleds. These land sleds were used rather than wagons in irregular, rocky areas where wheels were useless.

Profuse rhododendron provides campsite privacy. The 12 campsites are not overly large, but are great for those who love being creekside. A couple of water spigots serve the campground; there are two vault toilets up the hill away from Camp Creek. Remember, you must go to Mash Fork Campground to take a shower.

There is no set pattern to when this place fills, other than on summer holidays. Campsite capacity is very weather dependent, but you most likely can get a site at Blue Jay during the colder months. I recommend coming here during spring and fall. With little water recreation, it could get overly hot during the summer.

Just up Camp Creek from the campground is Campbell Falls. The water spills over a series of small ledges and gathers in a large pool. You can enjoy the waterfall after just a brief walk from your campsite. There is another waterfall up Farley Branch, which is a seasonal stream. You can take a foot trail from Blue Jay and walk to these falls, then either walk over toward Mash Fork or walk down alongside Farley Branch. All these streams can roar at times, and at other times barely trickle or even nearly dry up. But they are usually flowing pretty strongly in springtime, when the creeks get stocked with trout for anglers.

The rest of the trails are in the state forest. These paths follow old mountain roads through the broken woodland. Some of these are old railroad grades from the logging days. The area still has clearings from old farms and also designed clearings to enhance wildlife food production.

Use the park map to wind your way around here up creeks and along ridges. Many of the 20 miles of trails are used by mountain bikers. Slower-paced hikers may see wildlife here, most notably beaver, deer, and turkey. Faster-paced hikers may pass by a few things like old farm implements or a grouse. Camp Creek State Park and Forest is often passed by, other than interstate campers. However, other campers should be enjoying this forest, especially mountain bikers.

To get there: From Exit 20 on I-77, head south on U.S. 19 a short distance to Camp Creek Road (CR 19/5) and turn right. Follow Camp Creek Road for 2 miles to the state park and forest.

KEY INFORMATION

Camp Creek
P.O. Box 119
Camp Creek, WV 25820

Operated by: West Virginia State Parks

Information: (304) 425-9481, www.wvparks.com/campcreek

Open: Blue Jay: year-round; Mash Fork: April 1 through November 1

Individual sites: 26 electric, 12 nonelectric

Each site has: Picnic table, fire grate, lantern post

Site assignment: Reservations accepted, but not required

Registration: By phone, or park ranger will register you

Facilities: Hot showers, flush toilets, vault toilets, water spigots

Parking: At campsites only

Fee: $16 per night electric, $11 per night nonelectric

Elevation: 2,000 feet

Restrictions:

Pets—On leash only

Fires—In fire grates only

Alcoholic beverages—Prohibited

Vehicles—30-foot trailer limit

Other—14-day stay limit

GLADE CREEK

Beckley

The New River Gorge National River is the recreational centerpiece for this part of West Virginia. It is 53 miles of free-flowing water that runs mildly in some places and radically in others, creating paddling opportunities for canoeists, kayakers, and rafters alike. The steep gorge and smaller gorges on side creeks make for natural beauty that can also be enjoyed on foot. And where there is water, there are fish. In the area near the Glade Creek Campground, which is one of the gorge's finer tent campgrounds, fishing is good. And even if you don't catch any, the riverine forest at Glade Creek will raise your spirits. And if that doesn't do it, then remember how much it costs to camp here. Nothing.

Drive down to the end of dusty Glade Creek Road and turn into the campground. You are underneath a towering woodland of locust, river birch, buckeye, sycamore, and tulip trees. Other smaller versions of the same trees and more cover the forest floor, creating a dense forest so thick a greenhorn could get turned around inside of 50 yards away from his last known spot. Glade Creek tumbles down from the Appalachian Plateau behind you and the New River rumbles off in the distance.

Take the small road and come to the first campsite that provides a good sample of the drive-up campsites. It has a pull-through parking area and is culled from the lush growth around it. A picnic table, fire ring,

CAMPGROUND RATINGS

Beauty:	★★★★★
Site privacy:	★★★★★
Site spaciousness:	★★★★★
Quiet:	★★★★
Security:	★★★
Cleanliness/upkeep:	★★★★

The campground at Glade Creek is ideally situated for you to enjoy much of the gorge-ous scenery at this national river.

NEW RIVER VALLEY

and lantern post adorn the lightly graveled flat spot. The modern vault toilets are in an elaborate building off to your right. The next campsite has a wooden platform and offers disabled access. The remaining three drive-up sites are much like the first. Every one would satisfy even the most discriminating tent camper.

The walk-in tent sites are over by the river at the boat launch. Park your car and walk down the sand bar, shaded in river birch and sycamore, and pick one of the five marked campsites. There are great views of the river through the trees. Across the water are the CSX Railroad tracks, which run the length of the entire gorge. You'll find only rock fire rings at the walk-in tent sites, as this area occasionally gets flooded by the river and any tables and such would be washed away.

The drawback of this campground is its size. It will fill on nice weekends by Friday night. Come here early Friday if you are a weekend warrior. Luckily, there is a good campground just a few miles away. Just back on Glade Creek Road is the brand new Grandview Bar Campground. It has 20 drive-up camp-sites and 15 walk-in tent campsites.

Glade Creek offers good camping, good boating, and good fishing. A set of trails emanates from the campground. Just up from the campground was the old community of Hamlet. A trail leads upriver 0.3 mile to the site of the railroad bridge, whose construction caused the town to be here in the first place. The Glade Creek Trail follows an old railroad grade 5 miles up. There is good trout fishing along this stream. The stocked waterway is catch and release for the first 3 miles, and catch and keep after that. Glade Creek intersects the Kates Falls Trail to view a cascade. The Kates Plateau and Polls Plateau Trails follow old railroad grades. White blazes on trees mark the paths, but be careful, as these trails are hard to follow.

Anglers like to bank fish or get on the New in johnboats to vie for smallmouth bass, which are numerous. The swimming is good in the river, but life jackets are recommended by the park service. There is a solid current.

Another way to get on the New River is by canoe. The section of river from Hinton to Thurmond is class I–II with a few class III rapids. You can and should portage around two rough but pretty spots, Brooks Falls and Sandstone Falls. The 5-mile run from Glade Creek to Grandview Sandbar is a popular and convenient paddle from this campground.

Speaking of Grandview, above you is the Grandview Visitor Center, accessible via Beckley. At Grandview there is a good overlook, interpretive displays, and more park information. Also near here is the Cliffside Amphitheater featuring dramas, including *The Hatfields and McCoys*, which was played out in real life not too far from here to the southwest. Supplies are available nearby in Beckley. Go ahead and splurge, since the camping at Glade Creek is free.

To get there: From Beckley, take WV 41 north for 9 miles toward Prince. Turn right on Glade Creek Road just before crossing the bridge over the New River. Follow Glade Creek Road for 6 miles to dead-end at Glade Creek Campground.

KEY INFORMATION

Glade Creek Campground
P.O. Box 246
Glen Jean, WV 25846

Operated by: National Park Service

Information: (304) 465-0508, www.nps.gov/neri

Open: Year-round

Individual sites: 5 drive-up campsites, 5 walk-in tent sites

Each site has: Drive-up sites have picnic table, fire ring, lantern post; walk-in sites have fire ring

Site assignment: First come, first served; no reservations

Registration: Ranger will come by to register you

Facilities: Vault toilets; bring water

Parking: At campsites or tent camper parking area

Fee: None

Elevation: 1,400 feet

Restrictions:

   Pets—On leash only

   Fires—In fire rings only

   Alcoholic beverages—At campsites only

   Vehicles—None

   Other—14-day stay limit in 28-day period

GREENBRIER RIVER STATE FOREST

Lewisburg

Greenbrier State Forest relies on its natural qualities to attract most visitors. And well it should. The campground is nearly ideal in size and setting. The forest itself has activities for the self-motivated outdoors enthusiast, such as hiking and mountain biking, with other outdoor pursuits nearby. There are a few developed facilities, like a swimming pool. The famed Greenbrier River Trail is just a few miles away, and the Greenbrier River offers canoeing and fishing. West Virginia's most historic cave, Organ Cave, and nearby historic Lewisburg are definitely worth a visit. When you come back from whatever you are doing, the campground will seem like home.

Drive up along Harts Run and come to the campground on your right. Enter an area with five campsites beneath a thick forest of pine, maple, buckeye, oak, and hemlock. The spacious sites have a thick understory, which makes for good privacy. A small campground like this one never seems overly busy or crowded, even when it is full.

Turn right on an upper loop that houses nine campsites. Wooden borders delineate the shady campsites. Some of the sites are pull-up and others are pull-through. All the sites are desirable, even though those on this upper loop aren't perfectly level. However, tent pads have been installed in bumpier areas.

Leave the upper loop and pass two neat sites on their own little road. You may have trouble deciding which site to choose. The

CAMPGROUND RATINGS

Beauty:	★★★★
Site privacy:	★★★★
Site spaciousness:	★★★★
Quiet:	★★★★★
Security:	★★★★
Cleanliness/upkeep:	★★★★★

The small, attractive campground and slow pace make this a quiet mountain getaway for southeastern West Virginia.

NEW RIVER VALLEY

campground fills on Memorial Day weekend and two weekends in August: during the State Fair of West Virginia at Lewisburg and during the Civil War reenactment of the Battle at Dry Creek. Other than that, you should be able to get a campsite anytime, which is surprising, considering the quality and appeal of this campground, plus the few interstate travelers coming off I-64.

Hiking and biking trails at the state forest are centered around Kates Mountain, which dominates the landscape, and Harts Run, the stream that flows by the campground. The most challenging trek is the Kates Mountain Loop. Head up Rocky Ridge Trail to the top of Kates Mountain. Turn right and then walk along a forest road atop the ridge to drop down to Youngs Nature Trail. Return along Harts Run for an 8-mile circuit. There are overlooks atop Kates Mountain. Other shorter trails exist in the forest, but you may be lured to the Greenbrier River Trail. The southern terminus of this 75-mile rail trail is on the Greenbrier River near Caldwell. Mountain bikers love this path and you may see anglers vying for smallmouth bass.

The Greenbrier is also a good canoe float in season. Contact Woods, Water, and Wheels, located in downtown Lewisburg, at (888) 306-5539 for canoe rental and shuttle information. They also lead mountain-biking trips on Kates Mountain.

Lewisburg is a historic destination in its own right. There are many preserved buildings, and the downtown is a National Registered Historic District. Lewis Spring, which first brought settlement here, is preserved in a stone springhouse at Andrew Lewis Park. The Old Stone Church, the oldest continuously used church west of the Alleghenies, was built in 1796. The library and a Confederate cemetery are two other interesting sights. Take it all in with a walking tour of downtown.

Another historic walk can be found underground at Organ Cave. Thomas Jefferson visited this cavern, used extensively by the Confederates for saltpeter (used in making gunpowder). Take the regular tour or bring your old clothes for a lesser traveled, down-and-dirty, wild cave tour. There are brochures for Organ Cave at the state forest office. After this little adventure, you will certainly appreciate the showers back at Greenbrier State Forest.

To get there: From Lewisburg, drive east on I-64 for 6 miles to Exit 175. Turn right onto CR 60/14 and drive south for 2 miles to Greenbrier River State Forest.

KEY INFORMATION

Greenbrier River State Forest
HC 30, Box 154
Caldwell, WV 24925

Operated by: West Virginia State Parks

Information: (304) 536-1944, www.greenbriersf.com

Open: April 15 through October 31

Individual sites: 16

Each site has: Picnic table, stone fireplace, electricity, waste-water pit

Site assignment: Reservations accepted, but not required

Registration: By phone or ranger will come by and register you

Facilities: Hot showers, flush toilets, water spigots

Parking: At campsites only

Fee: $16 per night electric, $11 per night nonelectric

Elevation: 2,000 feet

Restrictions:

Pets—On leash only

Fires—In fireplaces only

Alcoholic beverages—Prohibited

Vehicles—30-foot trailer limit

Other—14-day stay limit

MONCOVE LAKE STATE PARK

Union

Moncove Lake lies at the most south-eastern edge of West Virginia's ridge and valley country, in the Sweet Springs Valley. In 1959, Devils Creek was dammed to make this mountain impoundment, which provides 144 acres of clear water ready for anglers and small boaters. Middle Mountain and Cove Mountain form scenic bastions overlooking Moncove Lake. Add a little development and a campground with one loop especially suited to tent camping and you have a true recreation destination.

Things don't get hopping at Moncove Lake until Memorial Day, when the campers really roll in, not only to enjoy the lake, but also the new swimming pool. The pool is set on the shores of Moncove Lake, offering a great view with all the conveniences of swimming in a man-made environment.

The campground has two loops. The right-hand loop, built on a partially forested slight slope, is bordered by two seasonal streams. This loop runs away from the lake, with the upper part shaded in pine trees. Its best attribute is a lake view from some of the campsites. That is because this loop is awfully open, though occasional maple trees dot the lower part. It also has electricity, which attracts the RVs that make it to Moncove. If you have any questions, the park office is oddly located in this loop. This may be the only park office I have seen in the middle of a campground

CAMPGROUND RATINGS

Beauty:	★★★★
Site privacy:	★★★
Site spaciousness:	★★★
Quiet:	★★★
Security:	★★★★★
Cleanliness/upkeep:	★★★★★

Moncove Lake is situated in a quiet mountain valley off the beaten path.

NEW RIVER VALLEY

loop. You will find the park staff very relaxed.

The left-hand loop is much better suited to tent camping. Pass from the open area into a hickory-oak forest, thickly canopied overhead, perched on a hilly area. The hills are not a detriment since the camp-sites have been leveled and the leveling adds to the scenery. White pine is more prevalent farther along the loop. The sites are average size and spread well apart. The loop drops down along Devils Creek, the outflow of Moncove

Lake. The five campsites strung out along Devils Creek are among the finest in the park. A water spigot and bathhouse are at the end of the loop.

Water recreation is the name of the game here. Moncove Lake holds trout, bass, bluegill, and catfish. People bank fish from the dam and at designated lake access areas. Others picnic along the lake. You'll find johnboats and pad-dleboats for rent, and if you bring your own boat remember that no motors over five horsepower are allowed.

Younger kids will enjoy the new pool built on the shores of Moncove Lake. Adults may want to take a dip after a hike on one of the park's many trails. The Devils Creek Trail leaves the left-hand camping loop and parallels Devils Creek. From here, you can turn right and make a loop with Diamond Hollow Trail, or loop around on the Roxalia Springs Trail. Organized sports are played on the park's ball field.

This is an easy-going park where relaxing, maybe watching a bobber at the end of your fishing line, is the most popular pastime. However, there are other attractions, such as the Greenbrier River and the Greenbrier River Rail Trail, to lure hikers, mountain bikers, and paddlers. You can fish the Greenbrier

River for bass, or take a relaxed float in a canoe. Organ Cave and Lost World Caverns offer underground tours, with a surprising amount of human history thrown in. When you come here, just make sure and camp in the good loop.

To get there: From Union, drive east on WV 3 for 9 miles to CR 8. Turn left on CR 8 and follow it for 6 miles to the state park, which will be on your left.

KEY INFORMATION

Moncove Lake State Park
Route 4, Box 73-A
Gap Mills, WV 24941

Operated by: West Virginia State Parks

Information: (304) 772-3450, www.wvparks.com/moncovelake

Open: April 1 through November 30

Individual sites: 25 electric, 25 nonelectric

Each site has: Picnic table, fire grate

Site assignment: First come, first served; no reservations

Registration: At campground check-in station

Facilities: Hot showers, flush toilets, water spigots

Parking: At campsites only

Fee: $16 per night electric, $11 per night nonelectric

Elevation: 2,500 feet

Restrictions:

Pets—On leash only

Fires—In fire grates only

Alcoholic beverages— Prohibited

Vehicles—None

Other—14-day stay limit

OHIO RIVER VALLEY

LEWIS WETZEL

New Martinsburg

L ewis Wetzel worked his way west through old Virginia in the late 1700s. It was a rough place—Indians still roamed freely about what later became West Virginia. Day-to-day living was dangerous. But this pioneer exemplified the courage and fortitude to survive in the wilderness he later made home. Wetzel County is home to this 12,000-acre wildlife management area, named in the pioneer's honor. You will find this place no longer as wild as Wetzel did, but it is a good place to come and camp and fish and hike.

The campground is in a scenic setting and boasts over 27 miles of trails, in addition to numerous jeep roads. The area, with elevations ranging from 700 to 1,500 feet in elevation, is managed for wildlife; you may see a critter or two. Be apprised this is a hunting zone. Call ahead to check dates so you can safely roam this pretty and rugged slice of northwest West Virginia.

After you drive up Buffalo Run, a side road splits off to the left. Putter through the woods, cross a bridge over a stream, then come to a pretty clearing surrounded by steep ridges on both sides. This is the confluence of Buffalo Run and Horse Run. The clearing is thick with green grass. Buffalo Run flows on your right. The campground begins. Pass the vault toilets and you'll find a string of campsites backed against the wooded creek. The campsites themselves are in the open for the most part. This

CAMPGROUND RATINGS

Beauty: ★★★★
Site privacy: ★★
Site spaciousness: ★★★★★
Quiet: ★★★★
Security: ★★★★
Cleanliness/upkeep: ★★★★

The trail-laced terrain here is as rugged as the legendary West Virginia pioneer for whom it was named.

OHIO RIVER VALLEY

could create a shade problem, but it does open up the view.

Wooden posts stuck in the ground delineate the campsites. The campsites are strung far apart, but the openness of the campground cuts down on camper privacy. Bring the big tent—spaciousness is no problem. Head on up to the top of the road; a turnaround houses some really large sites.

Campsites are available any time of the year, except for maybe the opening day of deer season. This may be a good place to come in winter to practice your cold weather camping skills. Late spring could be good too. High summer may be hot. Just call ahead to check for hunting dates.

Lewis Wetzel has some of the best hiking in this part of the state. The fishing isn't bad either. Trout are stocked in spring along the South Fork and North Fork Fishing Creek. South Fork Fishing Creek is known for its smallmouth bass. Good angling gave Fishing Creek its name. Anywhere along the road near Jacksonburg has good smallmouth populations.

The trails are what will keep you coming back. They run up the hollows and along the ridges here. I suggest hiking early or late to maximize your chances of wildlife viewing. The Horse Run Trail leaves from just below the campground and runs a mile to the High Knob Trail. You can turn left here and follow the Hart Trail to the Lesin Run Trail and down to Buffalo Run for a 3-mile loop.

For a longer loop, keep going on the High Knob Trail all the way to the Hiles Run Trail. Then drop down to Buffalo Run Road and return to the campground for a 7-mile circuit. Many other trails spur off the High Knob Trail for other loops. Get a trail map from the manager's office, which is conveniently located just down the road from the campground. This is also where the

Locust Trail starts and makes a 2.5-mile loop into the ridges. You will notice there are numerous, closed jeep roads on the west side of the area that are ripe for walking or biking.

Yet another trail leaves the campground and heads straight up Buffalo Run, with a side trail going up Meathouse Branch. I wonder what's up there? I guess I'll have to come back and find out.

To get there: From New Martinsburg, drive 23 miles east on WV 20 to the town of Jacksonburg. Turn right on Buffalo Run Road (CR 82) and cross South Fork Fishing Creek. Lewis Wetzel Wildlife Management Area is dead ahead.

KEY INFORMATION

Lewis Wetzel WMA
HC 62, Box 8
Jacksonburg, WV 26377

Operated by: West Virginia Division of Natural Resources

Information: (304) 889-3497, www.dnr.state.wv.us

Open: Year-round

Individual sites: 20

Each site has: Picnic table, fire grate

Site assignment: First come first served; no reservations

Registration: Self-registration on site

Facilities: Vault toilets; bring water

Parking: At campsites only

Fee: $5 per night

Elevation: 1,150 feet

Restrictions:

Pets—On leash only

Fires—In fire grates only

Alcoholic beverages—At campsites only

Vehicles—None

Other—14-day stay limit

McCLINTIC WILDLIFE MANAGEMENT AREA

Point Pleasant

Mc Clintic Wildlife Management Area is located in Mason County. And Mason County is nearly encircled by rivers, as the Ohio swoops and bends along the east, north, and west, and the Kanawha flows in from the south. McClintic itself lies near the confluence of the Ohio and Kanawha Rivers. A lot of water lies within the confines of McClintic—with over 30 lakes ready for the avid angler. Hunting is popular in season. But what really puts McClintic over the edge is the unusual campground. Imagine this: old, old trees, grassy fields, fishing ponds, and an awesome view of the cooling towers of Gavin Power Plant. The towers are a spectacle at night, too. Before coming here and seeing it for myself, I would have unequivocally said that viewing a power plant from a campsite would be not only a major detraction but an automatic elimination from this guidebook. But I found that this most unnatural sight actually enhanced my tent camping experience.

Before McClintic was a wildlife management area, it was a World War II munitions plant. And before that it was old farmland. Then, in 1950, the area was deeded to what is now the Division of Natural Resources. The DNR made wildlife plantings and constructed ponds for waterfowl and fish. And now McClintic has the greatest variety of wildlife habitats in any of the state's wildlife management areas. The old sugar

CAMPGROUND RATINGS

Beauty:	★★★
Site privacy:	★★★★
Site spaciousness:	★★★★★
Quiet:	★★★★
Security:	★★★★★
Cleanliness/upkeep:	★★★

With over 30 lakes, McClintic Wildlife Management Area is all about fishing and wildlife.

OHIO RIVER VALLEY

maples you see by the camping area were probably from
farmsteads.

After paying your modest $5
fee, roll down the gravel road
past the area manager's house
and come to the first camping
area. Off to your right, in a
grove of very old sugar
maples, are three shady campsites laid out in a semi-circle. A
grassy field lies along the road.
Woods lie between you and
Pond #3. A foot trail leads
from this camping area to the
pond. Off to the west are the
plant towers. The lone water

spigot is nearby. Ironically, the most used site, by far, is the one with the best
view of the towers.

Past this camping area is more of Pond #3 along the road, and just ahead is
the second camping area. The vault toilets are here. There are also some very
large trees that were here long before West Virginia became a state. The six
campsites are laid out in a row. The first three campsites are in the shade of
the ancient trees. The last three are out in the open. Fields extend beyond the
camping area. In fact, McClintic has 600 acres of farmland, 900 acres of brush-
land, 160 acres of wetlands, and 1,100 acres of mixed hardwood forest. This
diversity means a lot of wildlife. The birds were singing and the turkeys gob-
bling during my stay.

Hunting is popular here, and McClintic prides itself on catering to the phys-
ically disabled hunter with special duck blinds and deer stands. But most
enthusiasts come here for the fishing. No motorized craft are allowed on the
lakes and ponds, but canoes and craft with electric trolling motors are welcome. This makes for a peaceful fishing experience. Licensed anglers can vie

for bass and bluegill throughout the area. Channel catfish and northern pike are stocked in many ponds. Obtain an area map with the numerous roads and ponds from the park office. It is located near the campground. You can also inquire about what fish are at what pond and what ponds are open to fishing. Call ahead about hunting schedules.

There are a couple of nearby attractions. The West Virginia State Farm Museum is on the road to McClintic. Here you can see old farm buildings and implements and gain an understanding of what farming used to be like way back when. Back in Point Pleasant, where there are opportunities for supplies, is also the Point Pleasant Battlefield State Park. Here, a pre–Revolutionary War battle was fought between Indian tribes and Virginians that extended settler influence west to the Ohio River and later led to the westward extension of what became the United States. This park offers a great view of the confluence of the Ohio and Kanawha Rivers. I was glad to make this area part of my West Virginia tent-camping experience.

> To get there: From Point Pleasant, drive north on WV 62 for 5 miles, then turn right on CR 11 (Potters Creek Road) heading east. After 1.4 miles you'll see the McClintic Wildlife Management Area sign. Turn left at the first gravel road at the WMA sign and follow it for 0.2 mile. Turn left again at the sign for the WMA office and follow that gravel road for 0.2 mile, passing the park office. The campground will be ahead on your right.

KEY INFORMATION

McClintic WMA
Route 1, Box 484
Point Pleasant, WV 25550

Operated by: Division of Natural Resources

Information: (304) 675-4380, www.dnr.state.wv.us

Open: Year-round

Individual sites: 9

Each site has: Picnic table, stand-up grill

Site assignment: First come, first served; no reservations

Registration: Self-registration on site

Facilities: Pit toilets, water spigot

Parking: At campsites only

Fee: $5 per night

Elevation: 550 feet

Restrictions:

Pets—On leash only

Fires—In fire rings only

Alcoholic beverages—At campsites only

Vehicles—None

Other—No ATVs

NORTH BEND STATE PARK

Harrisville

North Bend State Park was here before the North Bend Rail Trail, but now the North Bend Rail Trail gets all the notoriety. This is one of the nation's most scenic and successful rail-to-trail conversions. The north bend referred to is a significant turn in the North Fork of Hughes River, which the trail follows and the park abuts. The rail to trail conversion began in 1989 and currently covers over 70 miles, running from near Parkersburg 27 miles to North Bend State Park and then east for another 43 miles to Wolf Summit. North Bend is not only an excellent place to enjoy this nationally acclaimed trail, but also for a little tent camping and more.

But just as the old Baltimore and Ohio Railroad is being changed from rail to trail, so is North Bend State Park changing. Acquired land and park expansion are leading to an additional campground, a lake with a beach, a new swimming pool, and equestrian trails that will make North Bend even better.

For now, the 47-site River Run Campground will do. And it will be the preferred place for tent campers in the future as well, for the new campground will have full hookups (read: RVs). Wind your way through the park and end up at River Run, on the banks of the North Fork of Hughes River. The first set of sites between the river and a fishing pond are shaded by sycamores and other creek-loving trees. You have your choice of camping along still

CAMPGROUND RATINGS

Beauty:	★★★
Site privacy:	★★★
Site spaciousness:	★★★★
Quiet:	★★★★
Security:	★★★★
Cleanliness/upkeep:	★★★★

The nationally acclaimed North Bend Rail Trail is the centerpiece of this park.

OHIO RIVER VALLEY

or moving water. The understory is mown grass.

Pass by the pond and come to the campground check-in station/store. Fishing equipment and a few supplies are here. A spur road near the check-in station has more tent campsites. The six pondside sites are great, but a little in the open. However, you can throw in a fishing line right from your tent. The sites away from the pond are on a slope and should be avoided.

Around the corner behind a hill are the electric sites. The

loop follows a bend in the North Fork of Hughes River. Twelve of the campsites are riverside. Some of the sites in the center of the loop are too open. Pass the bathhouse and there are more sites with adequate shade. This area is currently the domain of RVs because of the electricity. Some of these sites can be reserved.

Overall, the campground is appealing. There are good and bad sites. Be choosy. I like being by a river and a pond at the same time. The nonelectric sites are generally available. Just get here early if you plan to camp here on the Fourth of July or any other holiday.

Just across the North Fork of Hughes River, by a bridge, is the park trailhead for the North Bend Rail Trail. Bikers really enjoy the varied scenery on this path, from valleys to rural communities. Head east on the trail to traverse one of the 12 tunnels and 32 bridges that were once part of the B & O Railroad, constructed from 1853–1857. The rail bed has been made more user-friendly. There are three tunnels in the park vicinity. Bring your bike or rent one at the campground check-in station. Hikers and horseback riders are welcome, too.

Other standard trails are in the park, too. Check out the large rock formation on the Castle Rock Trail. The Giant Pine Trail heads through a grove of white pines. The Hibbs Cemetery Trail leaves the campground and climbs steeply to the Hibbs Family Cemetery. The Nature Trail is the park's most challenging. It forms a 4.5-mile loop and traverses varied terrain of the park, including along the Hughes River and up on rock outcrops of the high ridges. Don't be surprised if you see a deer. North Bend State Park is known for an abundance of does and bucks. Tired of walking? Fish in the pond or the river. Canoeing the North Fork Hughes River is popular, too.

The developed areas include tennis, volleyball, and miniature golf, all located near the North Bend Lodge, where you can get a good meal, if you tire of roasting hot dogs over the fire. Cool off in the park swimming pool.

The North Bend Rail Trail will probably always overshadow North Bend State Park, but the park does provide a good base camp to enjoy the rail trail and other sights of the park proper and area beyond.

To get there: From downtown Harrisville, drive west on Main Street (CR 5) for 4 miles and you will drive straight into the state park. The turn into the park and campground will be on your right.

KEY INFORMATION

North Bend State Park
Route 1, Box 221
Cairo, WV 26337

Operated by: West Virginia State Parks

Information: (304) 643-2931, www.northbendsp.com

Open: Mid-April through November 30

Individual sites: 26 electric, 21 nonelectric

Each site has: Picnic table, fire grate, stand-up grill

Site assignment: Reservations accepted, but not required

Registration: By phone, or at campground check-in station

Facilities: Hot showers, flush toilets, pay phone, laundry

Parking: At campsites only

Fee: $15 per night electric, $11 per night nonelectric

Elevation: 850 feet

Restrictions:

Pets—On leash only

Fires—In fire grates only

Alcoholic beverages—Prohibited

Vehicles—None

Other—14-day stay limit

TOMLINSON RUN STATE PARK

New Cumberland

The northern peninsula of West Virginia is unique. And where Tomlinson Run State Park lies, it is only 5 miles in either direction to the states of Ohio or Pennsylvania. West Virginia is lucky to have this pretty piece of our country. Tomlinson Run forms a valley where steep ridges make for mountainous terrain. And on top of one of these ridges is the park's campground. The heavily forested high ground gives a sense of being on top of the world, though the elevation is only 1,200 feet.

Actually, all around you is a fine state park, with some development tastefully added to the natural beauty of the area. Trails, a lake, fishing ponds, and a wilderness area are mixed with a huge pool, game courts, and picnic areas. So pack your tent and head on up to West Virginia's northernmost campground.

Wind your way up the ridge and come to the wooded camping area that splits in two directions along the ridge and is divided by the campground check-in station. To your left, south, is the Chief Big Foot Camping Area. This area is named after a seven-foot Indian who struggled with pioneers in the late 1700s, meeting his end where Tomlinson Run flows into the Ohio River, a mile below the state park.

At the campground, pass one of this park's unique characteristics, the Rent-a-camp. Here, you can not only get a campsite, but also a tent, cooler, stove, lantern,

CAMPGROUND RATINGS

Beauty:	★★★★
Site privacy:	★★★★
Site spaciousness:	★★★
Quiet:	★★★★★
Security:	★★★★
Cleanliness/upkeep:	★★★★★

This ridgetop campground in the state's northern peninsula is a worthy destination in itself.

OHIO RIVER VALLEY

and cookware to actually camp at the campsite. These six Rent-a-camp sites have cabin-style tents but no electricity. Past these sites are traditional campsites, separated by woods along the ridge, and the bathhouse for this area. A campground host is stationed near here for your safety and help.

Veer right around the small loop. Some of the sites are pull-through. Just past the loop is a spur road with the most secluded sites. These are among the ten campsites that can be reserved. The red maple and sugar maple–dominated forest drops off sharply below the campground, leaving a lot of sky above.

The Chief Logan Camping Area swings around the opposite side of the ridge. The first four campsites are nonelectric. The spacious sites are even more dispersed than the Chief Big Foot Area. Past the bathhouse, the gently rolling ridge dips down but soon levels again. A couple of sites are pull-through. A small turnaround area features five nonelectric sites that are the park's best. The ridge drops off sharply here, too.

Tomlinson Run can be busy. It fills nearly every weekend during high summer. Make reservations if you are coming from a long distance. It is sure to fill on big summer holidays. Once here, be sure to store your food. The raccoons are stealthy and persistent. They will eat your food unless it is properly put away.

Tomlinson Run is known for its swimming pool. It is Z-shaped and huge, as in able to accommodate 1,600 people. It also has a 182-foot, figure-eight water slide. Kids, have fun. Tennis courts and horseshoe pits are nearby. The park also went big building its miniature golf course.

There is other water besides the big pool. Four ponds are stocked with bass and bluegill. The North Fork and South Fork of Tomlinson Run have been dammed to form Tomlinson Run Lake. This impoundment also features fishing for bass, bluegill, channel catfish, and trout during the spring months. Rowboats and paddleboats are available for rent.

You can't ignore the amenities that drew both the Indians and the settlers to the Tomlinson Run region. The valleys and ridges are striking, as Tomlinson Run drops over 100 feet per mile en route to the Ohio River. Campers can enjoy many of the trails here by mountain bike or foot. The Poe Trail leaves the campground and heads to the fishing ponds or down to the South Fork to intersect the Big Foot Trail. Follow the Big Foot Trail along the lake to the new Half King Trail and return to the campground.

The prettiest location may be the park wilderness area. Follow the Laurel Trail down to the White Oak Trail and see the spring wildflowers, deep woods, and overhanging cliffs. Fall is especially colorful. It was just below this area that the settlers traced Chief Big Foot by his namesake footprints, which led to the encounter on the banks of the Ohio between Andre Poe and Chief Big Foot. Now the times have changed and the story is a West Virginia legend. Make some memories of your own up here in the northern panhandle.

To get there: From New Cumberland, take WV 2 north to WV 8. Drive east on WV 8 north for 3 miles to the state park entrance, which will be on your left.

KEY INFORMATION

Tomlinson Run State Park
P.O. Box 97
New Manchester, WV 26056

Operated by: West Virginia State Parks

Information: (304) 564-3651, www.wvparks.com/tomlinsonrun

Open: April 1 through October 31

Individual sites: 39 electric, 15 nonelectric

Each site has: Picnic table, fire grate, lantern post

Site assignment: Reservations accepted, but not required

Registration: By phone, or campground check-in station

Facilities: Hot showers, flush toilets, water spigot, pay phone, coin laundry

Parking: At campsites only

Fee: $16 per night electric, $11 per night nonelectric, $22 per night Rent-a-camp

Elevation: 1,200 feet

Restrictions:
  Pets—On leash only
  Fires—In fire grates only
  Alcoholic beverages—Prohibited
  Vehicles—None
  Other—14-day stay limit

APPENDICES

APPENDIX A
Camping Equipment Checklist

Except for the large and bulky items on this list, I keep a plastic storage container full of the essentials for car camping so they're ready to go when I am. I make a last-minute check of the inventory, resupply anything that's low or missing, and away I go!

Cooking Utensils
Bottle opener
Bottles of salt, pepper, spices, sugar, cooking oil and maple syrup in waterproof, spillproof containers
Can opener
Corkscrew
Cups, plastic or tin
Dish soap (biodegradable), sponge and towel
Flatware
Food of your choice
Frying pan, spatula
Fuel for stove
Lighter, matches in waterproof container
Plates
Pocketknife
Fire starter
Pot with lid
Stove
Tin foil
Wooden spoon

First Aid Kit
Band-Aids
First aid cream
Gauze pads
Aspirin
Insect repellent
Moleskin
Sunscreen/chapstick
Tape, waterproof adhesive

Sleeping Gear
Pillow
Sleeping bag
Sleeping pad, inflatable or insulated
Tent with ground tarp and rainfly

Miscellaneous
Bath soap (biodegradable), wash cloth and towel
Camp chair
Candles
Cooler
Deck of cards
Flashlight/headlamp
Paper towels
Plastic zip-top bags
Sunglasses
Toilet paper
Water bottle
Wool blanket

Optional
Barbecue grill
Binoculars
Field guides on bird, plant, and wildlife identification
Fishing rod and tackle
Lantern
Maps (road, trail, topographic, etc.)

APPENDIX B
Information

Monongahela National Forest
200 Sycamore Street
Elkins, WV
(304) 636-1800, www.fs.fed.us/r9/mon/

West Virginia Department of Tourism
2101 Washington Street East
P.O. Box 50312
Charleston, WV 25305-0312
(800) CALLWVA, (304) 225 5982, www.callwva.com

West Virginia State Parks and Forests
State Capitol Complex, Building 3, Room 709
Charleston, WV 25305
(800) CALLWVA, (304) 558-2764, www.callwva.com

West Virginia Division of Natural Resources
State Capitol Complex, Building 3, Room 669
Charleston, WV 25305-0660
(304) 558-2754, www.dnr.state.wv.us

New River Gorge National River
P.O. Box 246
Glen Jean, WV 25846
(304) 465-0508, www.nps.gov/neri

U.S. Army Corps of Engineers
Recreation Resources Branch
502 8th Street
Huntington, WV 25701
(304) 529-5607

George Washington National Forest
109 Molineau Road
Edinburgh, VA 22834
(540) 984-4101, www.fs.fed.us/gwjnf

ABOUT THE AUTHOR

J ohnny Molloy is an outdoor writer based in Knoxville, Tennessee. His outdoor life began on a backpacking trip into the Great Smoky Mountains National Park. That first trip, though a disaster, unleashed an innate love of the outdoors that has led to his spending over 100 nights per year in the wild, over the past 15 years, backpacking and canoe camping throughout our country and abroad. Specifically, he has spent over 650 nights in the Smokies alone, where he cultivated his woodsmanship and expertise on those lofty mountains. He has been an adopt-a-trail volunteer in the Great Smoky Mountains National Park for several years. Little Bottoms Trail is the trail he maintains.

In 1987, after graduating from the University of Tennessee with a degree in economics, he continued to spend an ever-increasing time in the natural places, becoming more skilled in a variety of environments. Friends enjoyed his adventure stories, and one even suggested he write a book. Soon he was parlaying his love of the outdoors into an occupation.

The results of his efforts are ten books: *Day & Overnight Hikes in the Great Smoky Mountains National Park* (Menasha Ridge Press, 1995), *Trial by Trail: Backpacking in the Smoky Mountains* (University of Tennessee Press, 1996), *The Best in Tent Camping: The Southern Appalachian and Smoky Mountains* (Menasha Ridge Press, 1997), *The Best in Tent Camping: Florida* (Menasha Ridge Press, 1998), *Day & Overnight Hikes in Shenandoah National Park* (Menasha Ridge Press, 1998), *Beach & Coastal Camping in Florida* (University Press of Florida, 1999), *The Best in Tent Camping: Colorado* (Menasha Ridge Press, 1999), *Paddler's Guide to Everglades National Park* (University Press of Florida, 2000), *The Best in Tent Camping: West Virginia* (Menasha Ridge Press, 2000), *Day & Overnight Hikes in the Monongahela National Forest* (Menasha Ridge Press, 2000).

Molloy has also written numerous magazine articles. The *Day & Overnight Hikes* books are guidebooks, each containing 42 recommended hikes that take the reader on a detailed journey to infrequently visited sites, from highland meadows and open vistas to pristine mountain streams and pioneer farms in the Appalachians. Of those 42 hikes, 22 are there-and-back day hikes, 10 are day-loop hikes, and 10 two-night overnight loops for the weekend backpacker. *Trial by Trail* is a narrative, a collection of 14 real-life backpacking adventure stories that weave Smokies facts and lore along with practical backpacking tips and glimpses of Molloy's growth as a woodsman. *The Best in Tent Camping* books parlay his vast camping experiences throughout the Southern Appalachians, Colorado, West Virginia, and Florida into concise guides of the 50 best tent campgrounds in each area offering the finest scenery and recreational opportunities the South and Rockies have to offer. *Beach & Coastal Camping in Florida* details the 24 best oceanside camping sites for tent, pop up, and RV campers.

Paddler's Guide to Everglades National Park includes detailed descriptions of all the commonly paddled routes and campsites in the Everglades and helpful information for paddlers who explore the backcountry. It includes over 50 photos.

Molloy continues to write and travel extensively to all four corners of the United States endeavoring in a variety of outdoor pursuits. For the latest updates on Johnny Molloy, check out his Web site at www.johnnymolloy.com.

I n d e x